All Services, All the Time

All Services, All the Time

*How Business Services Serve
Your Business*

Doug McDavid

BUSINESS EXPERT PRESS

All Services, All the Time: How Business Services Serve Your Business

First published in 2016 by
Business Expert Press, LLC
222 East 46th Street, New York, NY 10017
www.businessexpertpress.com

ISBN-13: 978-1-63157-276-0 (paperback)
ISBN-13: 978-1-63157-277-7 (e-book)

Business Expert Press Service Systems and Innovations in Business and Society Collection

Collection ISSN: 2326-2664 (print)
Collection ISSN: 2326-2699 (electronic)

Cover and interior design by Exeter Premedia Services Private Ltd., Chennai, India

First edition: 2016

10 9 8 7 6 5 4 3 2 1

Printed in the United States of America.

Abstract

This book takes the position that organizations, such as businesses and government agencies, form a special class of living system. As such they come into being, live through lifecycle stages, and can experience organizational health and various forms of organizational illness along the way. If the latter is frequent or extended, such organizations often die an untimely death. A services perspective can go a long way to combat this outcome and assist in maintaining organizational health. Allowing this perspective to permeate an organization induces a consideration of its genuine value and leads to a greater understanding of the breadth of stakeholders who are the beneficiaries of it. Productivity and services in an organization are symbiotic and must be so in order to achieve the balance that is key to the health of each organization. A services perspective illuminates as well the pivotal role that business-to-business service providers play in ensuring that balance is achieved and maintained. This book explores these factors from the point of view of the business leader and anyone concerned with the health of any organization.

Keywords

B2B services, business culture, business diagnostics, business health, business language, business leaders, living enterprise, organization leaders, service innovation, services

Contents

Preface

This book is written in second person, addressing "you" pretty much throughout. It's a fair question to ask, "Who is this 'you' that you're talking to?" I have in mind, generally, the owner of a business when I address "you." This book provides insights and questions to help a business owner think through the opportunities and complications of leading an organization into the unknown future.

Having said that, this book can be useful to a very wide audience indeed. People who lead nonprofit and public organizations face many of the same challenges as profit-making businesses. People who are not yet running a business often aspire to start a business at some point in their lives. And today, many people view a career as a business or an enterprise in its own right. In addition, all those professionals who provide consulting, coaching, and architecture services to support the health of businesses can find important concepts to help them, both with their own businesses and with the work they do with clients.

Acknowledgments

I want to thank the following people for valuable help in exploring the ideas in this book. I may not have followed all of your advice, but I am grateful for your thoughts. Including those of you for whom this acknowledgment probably comes as a surprise!

Erik Jan Abels, Gabriel Acosta-Mikulasek, Mary Adams, David Arella, Ajay Asthana, Ron Baker, JD Beckingham, Lori Bell, Rob Benjamin, Peter Bishop, Sharron Bradley, Dave Britton, Peter Burgess, Marty Burns, Erik Bush, Darryl Carr, Butch Casanova, Melissa Cefkin, Betty Jo Chang, Luba Cherbakov, Joris Claeys, Paul Daly, Niklas Damiris, Jimena Davila, Dolores Davis, Larry Davis, Haluk Demirkan, Sudhir Desai, Lia DiBello, Mark Dixon, Deborah Dunagan, Geoff Elliott, Roger Evernden, Len Fehskens, Lance Fowler, Janey Conkey Frazier, Adam Frick, Seth Fulk, Glen Gage, Diane Garga, Marc Gewertz, Martin Gladwell, Pat Gongla, Tom Graves, Ben Gray, Steve Haeckel, Jana Hamel, Debora Hammond, Karen Harvey, Hunter Hastings, Matt Hettinger, Trevor Hilder, Larry Hiner, Niranjan Hiras, Ralph Hodgson, Patrick Hoverstadt, Don Hutcheson, Robert Imrisek, David Ing, Larry Johnson, Dave Kamalsky, Raj Kasarabada, Sandy Kearney, Chris King, Janice Knight, Michael Kramer, Steve Kwan, "Max" Kathleen Latham, Brian Lee, Allenna Leonard, Brian Lucas, Skip Lumley, Paul Maglio, Steve Marcus, Michael Martine, Lisa Marie Martinez, Humberto Maturana, Mike McClintock, Amanda McDavid, Carleen McDavid, Bruce McNaughton, Yassi Moghaddin, Panda Morgan, Doug Morse, Bogdan Motoc, Sara Moulton-Reger, Peter Murchland, Pascal Negros, Cameron Norman, Tricia O'Keefe, Ken Orr, Karl Palachuk, John Palmer, Sukanya Patwardhan, Jim Pelley, Guy Rackham, Ram Ramanathan, Lynn Reyes, Jack Ring, Denis Roberts, Roy Roskilly, Pallab Saha, Jim Salmons, Jorge Sanz, Jeff Saperstein, Rahul Saxena, Kevin Smith, David Spellmeyer, Dean Spitzer, Jim Spohrer, Mike Straka, Ray Strong, Anders Tell, Andrey Tikhonov, Colin Tong, Jennifer Trelewicz, Dave Tryon, Chris Wagner, Art Warmoth, Howard Wiener, Helga Wild, Mike Wing, Catherine Winters, Irving

Wladawsky-Berger, Allen Woods, Julia Kious Zabell, Michael Zepponi, Tim Zerbiec, Berry Zimmerman, Marla Zorn, and Randy Zorn.

Of course I hold myself responsible for any issues that result from me not listening well enough! And great apologies to the people I have inevitably omitted from this acknowledgment of gratitude.

Introduction

This book asks you to look at your business in ways that may be unexpected or uncomfortable to your normal ways of thinking about things. The overarching idea is that no matter what you do, no matter what your business is designed to accomplish, your business can be legitimately and entirely viewed as a web of services. Additionally, your business, and in fact all human organizations, exist as *living* systems, with birth to death lifecycles, and with various levels of health along the way. Consequently, what we will cover in this book focuses on organizations as living webs of services.

How does that strike you? Do you find that perspective new, and a bit unnerving? Or perhaps you already think in these terms, and are entirely comfortable with that thought.

Starting from the living web of services perspective, the book makes the case that all organizations are defined by the co-creation of value through the services they *deliver*, and structured by *internal* webs of services. We articulate those webs of internal and external services as structures of service-roles, role-players, and networks of roles.

This book is divided into four main parts. The first part explores the hopes and dreams of business founders, owners, and leaders, and why it can be so difficult to realize the dream. We examine the sheer complexity of business, and all the moving parts that must operate together. We focus in on the challenge of leading an entity that takes on a life and a mind of its own in a very real way.

The second part explores ways to think about a business as a living web of services, with a structure of service-roles, role-players, and service-nets. We apply that structure to several layers of organization, including leadership. We differentiate three classes of service:

- Services performed by your business for co-creation of value with external stakeholders
- Services performed within your business, forming the internal structure
- Services that you engage to promote the health of your business

The third part explores several approaches to the diagnosis of healthy and unhealthy businesses. We examine a coaching approach, review the functionality that's simply required to remain in business, contrast that with the need to maintain a certain level of stability. We also introduce a sampling of tried and true business frameworks as diagnostic tools and then update those frameworks with a few more recent perspectives. And we look at the complexity of many cultures and many languages of business, as a way of providing insight into business health.

Finally, the fourth part explores a number of ways to maintain a healthy balance by using internal-facing services, as well as the types of health-promoting business-to-business services available for you to call upon.

So let's get started by taking a look at a few of the factors that make it so hard to succeed in business, even though we're really trying.

PART I

The Illusion of Control

CHAPTER 1

Business Dreams and Hard Realities

Starting and running a business is always an adventure. Even for seasoned entrepreneurs, every new venture requires a step into the unknown, because each business is unique and every situation is unique. But whether it's a for-profit, a nonprofit, an NGO, or a government agency being stood-up under another agency, a new venture always starts with some kind of a dream.

Maybe it was the dream of independence. Maybe it was the dream of becoming wealthy. Maybe it was the dream of making a contribution to society or the community. Maybe it was the dream of doing what you love, only what you love, and having fun doing it.

The so-called American Dream is all about quitting your job, getting out from under the control of the boss, and running your own business. Those of you who have done that may nod sagely, and say, "Yes, but it's not so easy …"

The life of an entrepreneur is exciting and totally involving. Everyone expects the 24 x 7 focus on getting a business off the ground. But people do not necessarily expect that two or three years later, even when there is money coming in and the business is thriving, the life of the business owner and founder can still be totally dominated by the business.

Rags to Riches

Everybody knows rags-to-riches stories about some amazing entrepreneur, or the lean startup that upturned an entire industry, or the founder who made 100 losing pitches for funding before finally hitting the jackpot.

My personal favorite story comes from a business I consulted with for a year. This business started very simply with a husband and wife team running it on their dining room table with paper index cards. A key moment in the history of this company came after it had become an industry-leader, and the couple decided to divorce. Everyone assumed the husband would buy out the wife, but instead, she bought him out. Years later, in the midst of the contract I was working, the company was sold—for a cool one billion dollars! From the dining table to billionaire—quite an adventure! And an image of how a business dream can lead to truly amazing results.

The problem is, no such success is guaranteed. There are plenty of scary statistics on how many startups fail in the first year, how many fail in the first five years, how many fail before being funded through an IPO or before being acquired.

Striving for Complexity

This harsh reality is built into the very nature of business. Business is all about shaping the resources of a generally chaotic world so as to bring forth interesting, useful, and valuable results. Building and leading a business requires maintaining a healthy balance between chaos, on the one hand (with high uncertainty and randomness), and, on the other hand, excessive control (with tight, rigid, and fragile constraints). The goal is to remain in the sweet spot of healthy complexity (adaptive, innovative, and productive) (Clippinger 1999).

Many Moving Parts

The difficulty of bringing sustainable value out of chaos starts with the sheer number of diverse activities that your business needs to attend to on a daily basis. To succeed in business, you (or *someone*) absolutely must pay attention to all of the following aspects:

- Developing a vision and strategy
- Developing and managing products and services
- Marketing and selling products and services
- Delivering products and services

- Managing customer service
- Developing and managing human capital
- Managing information technology
- Managing financial resources
- Acquiring, constructing, and managing assets
- Managing enterprise risk, compliance, and resiliency
- Managing external relationships
- Developing and managing business capabilities

This list is based on a common, standardized classification of business processes (APQC 2014). In the APQC framework, each of these categories is decomposed four or five levels. At the lower levels of this generic hierarchy, there are around 1,000 potential process concerns. And that's not to mention the many versions of this hierarchy that have been created for specific industries. Maybe your business is simple enough not to have to attend to all 1,000. However, even at the fourth level of decomposition we find important issues such as "2.1.5.1 Introduce new products/services" and "3.3.1.3 Generate sales forecast." This makes it clear that there are tons of issues to be understood and addressed. It's easy to see how the sheer magnitude of work in running any business can be overwhelming.

As if that weren't enough, you know very well that it's possible, even likely, to overshoot, and bring *too much* order to the situation. It's all too easy to end up trapped in a very brittle, overly controlling attempt to micromanage every aspect of your business. As you try to move forward, you find yourself experiencing analysis paralysis. You believe that the only way the business can move is if *you* move it. But then you find yourself frozen in place, like a deer in the headlights.

What was that dream that got you going? What is the dream that gets you up in the morning? How is it working out for you now?

Growing Pains

How would you define a healthy business? Do you even think in those terms? I mean, do you think about a business as something that can be healthy or unhealthy?

Many owners and managers of businesses, all the way up to huge multinationals, *do* think in terms of the health of their businesses. They think in terms of life and death of the business. During my years in IBM I became used to hearing top-level executives talk about the "near-death experience" IBM faced, when challenged by the PC revolution, and all that came with it.

It is not necessary to reach the point of "near death" before experiencing some, or many, of the following common kinds of pain:

- Lack of time
- Lack of money
- Lack of growth
- Low profits
- Declining sales
- High costs
- Taxes
- Burdensome regulations
- Low morale
- High rates of absenteeism and turnover
- Troublesome employees
- Fractured leadership team

A healthy business does not happen automatically, or by chance. It happens by working effectively ON the business.

> Once you recognize that the purpose of your life is not to serve your business, but that the primary purpose of your business is to serve your life, you can then go to work on your business, rather than in it, with a full understanding of why it is absolutely necessary for you to do so. (Gerber 2009)

At a minimum, this requires you, the leader of the business, to develop a bit of a CEO mindset—to become the true leader of the business, not merely the star performer. This is *not* to say that you, as the leader, must abandon the passion for what got you into the business. This is not an either-or situation, but rather a balance.

Table 1.1 Leadership balance

both this ...	and this ...
Strategic marketing	Effective selling
Exploiting things that are already under control	Exploring fresh opportunities
Rising to challenges	Conquering the routine
Creating and communicating a compelling vision	Steering a steady course
Creating a simple, understandable plan	Executing against that plan
Being adaptive	Leveraging efficiencies

Other balance points include the need to accomplish the following as seen in Table 1.1.

You need to balance a system that works with people you can trust to work the system. We will think about how to replace trial and error management with real business-craft that balances tried and true methods with 21st century technology and culture. We will examine a range of tools and techniques that help you lift the burden of the day-to-day issues off your shoulders so that you can accomplish this balancing act.

Getting Past Blind Spots

One of the key issues is that, as much as you know, there are always important things that you don't know, and even worse, things that you don't even know that you don't know. These are the dreaded blind spots that we all have, simply as human beings.

- You think there's a problem with your website, but it's really poor market research.
- You think the problem is pricing, but it's really poor service design.
- You think there's a customer mismatch, but it's really poorly trained employees.
- You think its hiring practices, but it's really lack of communication between managers and employees.
- You think it's the younger generation of slackers, but it's actually uncompetitive pay rates.

- You think it's poor training, but it's really inappropriate job design.
- You think it's lack of discipline, but it's really that employees do not feel valued.

Get the Picture?

The bottom line is to establish a system of habits of thought and action designed to achieve and maintain the balance needed for a healthy business. But before we can get there, we first need to take a deeper look at why it feels like your business has a life of its own, and a mind of its own.

CHAPTER 2

Living Organizations

So far we have established that the dream of business ownership and leadership can all too often turn into a mixed blessing, or even a nightmare. We have seen that a part of the reason is the sheer number of moving parts involved in running a business. But that's not all, and may not even be the most important issue you face in leading your business.

If you remember nothing else about this book, I hope you will take away this key point: The starting point for building and growing a healthy business (or any organization) is the recognition that your business is actually alive. Let me repeat—your business is truly and fundamentally a living thing. As such it has an existence apart from you. In other words, it actually *does* have a life of its own. In the next chapter we will explore the process of how this life form comes into existence. For the moment, though, let's take a quick look at the implications of this "fact of life," by examining parallel patterns of different classes of living things as well as key factors that need to be kept in balance.

Biological and Organizational Life

Here's a compare-and-contrast list of some key characteristics of life, assembled from several definitions of life itself.* You can see how these apply in different ways to both organic and business life (biological and organizational). Every form of life undergoes a basic lifecycle, which starts with an emergence phase, followed by some period of sustainment, and leads ultimately to disintegration. Emergence and sustainment of a living system, any living system, requires the following abilities:

---

* This list was compiled for a presentation to the International Society of Systems Sciences in 2008. Without footnoting every single point, which often came from several sources, the authors consulted include: Erwin Schrödinger, Robert Rosen, Ludwig von Bertalanffy, Lynn Margulis, James Grier Miller, Humberto Maturana and Francisco Varela, Stafford Beer, and Niklas Luhmann.

Table 2.1 Requirements for biological and organizational life

Life requirement	Biological	Organizational
The ability to *emerge from a codified design*	Both organisms and organizations have the ability to emerge from a codified design. In the case of biological organisms this design is encoded in DNA molecules.	In organizations, including your business, the codified design exists in founding documents that established the corporation, partnership, or public sector institution. These documents are structured by laws and regulations that govern the formation of organizations.
The ability to *maintain an identity over time*	Having once emerged into being, an instance of a biological life form (plant, animal, and especially human being) has an identity that is maintained over time. You are you, as an organism, from the time you were born until now, even though you have undergone uncountable changes, and replaced a high percentage of the cells in your body many times over. Even if you change your name, you remain you, as the same identifiable self.	The identity of an organization can remain surprisingly resilient even as its participating members come and go. We see this situation over and over in acquisitions of one business by another. The name change of the one is not enough to change its identity overnight. The effort to truly change the identity of an acquired business very often leads to strife, and even failure to achieve the desired results. Some organizational identities have endured over very long time periods. Think of the Catholic Church, which has maintained its identity for centuries as an organization, an institution, and yes, even a business.
The ability to *respond to stimuli*	Viability requires the ability to perceive opportunities and threats, the ability to process the implications of such perceptions, and the ability to form intent and take actions.	A key point for your business is to recognize that nearly every participant may experience important stimuli. Successful organizations are the ones that effectively tap into those sources of information, and then respond effectively.
The ability to *metabolize*	Here we're talking about input, processing, and output systems. Biological metabolism is a matter of physical inputs and processing of food, water, and oxygen provides input for their metabolism.	Businesses metabolize a whole range of tangible and intangible things. All this input must be sorted out, and hopefully turned into something of value. The tangibles are largely consumed in the process of creating physical artifacts, where intangibles form the truly living aspects of the business or organization.

The ability to *grow* (*within limits*)	In the case of animals and plants, nature has supplied the ability to grow to a certain size, and then imposes limits to growth (so that we don't expect to see 300 pound mice).	Organizations have pressures to maintain continual growth, but major changes occur as they grow beyond certain thresholds. This has strong linkage to communication, as larger numbers of people need to be in clear agreement on more complicated issues.
The ability to *self-regenerate*	Biological systems have natural mechanisms to repair physical damages. Mostly this is at the cellular level, but some animals can even regrow, for instance, a replacement claw or leg. Neuroplasticity in the brain is an important regenerative process, and medical science can now augment that process with stem cells.	An organization can replace individual role-players, and can even regenerate a whole department (IT, for instance) that decides to spin off into a company on its own. This is similar to neuroplasticity of the human brain, which enables healthy areas to assume functions of damaged areas. We might think of a newly hired employee as the equivalent of a regenerating stem cell for the business.
The ability to *self-regulate*	We see this in the internal forces that cause an organism to breathe on a regular basis, to respond to hunger and thirst by the pursuit of nourishment, the ability to slough off excess heat or seek heat sources to stave off excessive cold.	One way to look at self-regulation in the organization is through the checks and balances of different departments and disciplines internally (e.g, accounting that balances R&D, legal that balance sales). This organizational self-regulation includes passing down external regulation from various jurisdictions.
The ability to *manage variety*	Management of variety is an important aspect of keeping an organism well enough to function effectively. The problem with variety arises in the form of unexpected threats. An animal needs to be prepared to fend off predators and rivals. But an unexpected toxin may be a form of variety that the animal is totally unprepared to address.	Management of variety can become extremely complicated in the case of business, where threats come from unexpected sources, including sources that actually harbor carefully disguised intentions to dislodge you from your niche. One way to think about variety management is that the business can institute homeostatic mechanisms that deflect or reduce external disruptions, while enhancing the abilities of the organization to modify the activity of the external environment.

(Continued)

Table 2.1 Requirements for biological and organizational life (Continued)

Life requirement	Biological	Organizational
The ability to *maintain relationships*	Biological systems require the ability to maintain their physical integrity—the relationships among their various parts. Many also evolve symbiotic relationships with other species.	For businesses, this presents special problems, when the needed relationships are with autonomous individuals and organizations, including employees, customers, and suppliers. The rate of turnover and evolution can be relatively rapid in comparison to biology.
The ability to *form a purpose*	Both biological and social systems must have the ability to form and pursue goals. The difference is that an individual person or animal forms purposes at the individual level, which can be activated and pursued by the individual. Organizations deal with purposefulness of individuals *as well as* group purpose.	"A social system has purposes of its own; so do its parts, and so do the systems that contain it and the other systems they contain. A social system floats in a sea of purposes at multiple levels with some purposes incompatible within and between levels; and its management must concern itself with all of these." (Ackoff 1981, 2003) The lack of common purpose among individuals and the group can be one of the greatest sources of an unhealthy business.
The ability to *decide*	Based on the imperatives of their individual purpose and perceived information about conditions from the environment, individuals decide on what they believe to be advantageous courses of action.	"Decision makers carry the responsibility to familiarize themselves with the business context and decision model, and work with the decision process to arrive at the best decisions for the business" (Saxena and Srinivasan 2012). Often requirements for "buy-in" decisions can affect the organization's health for better or for worse.
The ability to *communicate*	In biology, the nervous system communicates throughout the body, as does the immune system, via the circulatory system. There are elaborate communication systems among members of a species, from the humpback whale, to flocks of birds, and herds of prey animals on the savannah.	In the case of organizations, communication occurs through contact among autonomous players, using more and more varied channels. This includes communication within the organization and outward into the marketplace. Considerations of business health revolve around the effectiveness of communications, which become ever more important in a networked, global, business environment.

The ability to *reproduce*	Of course, organisms reproduce, and in nature, the reproductive methods show a great deal of interesting variety, from bacteria that reproduce by simply dividing to various forms of sexual reproduction.	The standard business form of reproduction is the startup, with the special class of franchises. For business and other organizations, there are even more mechanisms including various forms of division and combination, mergers, acquisitions, spin-outs, and so on.
The ability to *learn*	The ability to learn is somewhat variable among members of a species, and even more variable across species borders. In general, behaviors are hard-wired in genetics and evolve over generations. Human beings have broken through to a unique level of learning ability, which makes us "time-binders" in our ability to learn from each other, and from records left by previous generations (Korzybski 2014).	The ability to achieve organizational learning is one of the greatest sources of excellent health or business illness. As Peter Senge said, "The only sustainable competitive advantage is an organization's ability to learn faster than the competition" (Senge 1990). Arie De Geus echoes, "The ability to learn faster than your competitors may be the only sustainable competitive advantage" (DeGeus 1997). We might be tempted to say that the learning organization is a healthy organization!
The ability to *adapt*	Genetic adaptations at the species level are quite slow, and adaptation at the individual level is limited to what is programmed into the individual by genetics, including such factors as seasonal variations.	Human beings have an almost infinite ability to adapt to situations, and this ability is largely a result of collective behavior via organizations. You, as the leader of an organization, can have a major effect on limiting or enabling the organization to adapt to changing circumstances (Haeckel 1999).

Life as a Balancing Act

In addition to the generic functionality required to emerge and sustain biological and organizational life, there are many balancing mechanisms required for healthy life. A few of these balance points (not either–or, but both–and) are listed in Table 2.2, and then explained below.

Every living being has a boundary and is embedded in an environment. In the case of an animal, the boundary is a skin, with elaborations like hair, feathers, a shell, and so on. For a business, the boundary is not so clear-cut, but you can probably think of how this works. Most businesses worry about information that is guarded as proprietary and valuable assets they don't want stolen. There are facilities (offices, warehouses) that are kept under lock and key for protection from intruders. One of the issues with a business is that this boundary is not fully physical, so it is not as obvious as in the case of an animal.

Every living system attempts to maintain a level of stability within flows of material, energy, and information. Too little food or water, and an animal will die. At the same time, too much water, and a land-dwelling organism will drown. For an organization, being cut off from a key source of supply can jeopardize its viability, as can a lack of cash flow. At the same time, when a flow becomes overpowering, it can upset the stability to the point that the living entity disintegrates. Fortunately for us in this time of information explosion, information flows are not usually directly fatal. But they can be disruptive and disorienting, creating unhealthy conditions that through distraction can lead to injury or death from other forces.

A characteristic of all biological and social living systems concerns the balance between independence and interdependence. Both animals and plants depend on nutrients, water, and light to varying degrees. They also depend upon other species in their ecosystems for food, to pollinate,

Table 2.2 Balancing mechanisms

Maintain a boundary	within	an environment
Maintain stability	amidst	flows
Sustain independence	and	interdependence
Pursue competition	alongside	cooperation

and to break down waste. In this regard, humans as organisms have taken great leaps forward in independence through the inventiveness and skill of making tools and shaping environments that take relatively independent control of providing the conditions required for life within otherwise very hostile conditions. To accomplish, for instance, life in outer space, people depend significantly on other people, effectively substituting one form of dependence for another. This explains our focus on relatively stable (dependable) groups. From the organizational perspective, those groups, in turn develop both dependencies, and independence of their own. For instance, a startup company is initially totally dependent on its founder(s), but over time must become founder-independent, while still depending on a growing set of skills, as well as resources of many kinds. A company that remains dependent on the founder risks jeopardizing its own health and the health of the founder as well.

Both biological life and organizational life involve balancing between cooperation and competition. In the ecosystem view of organisms, there is clearly competition for the basics of life, but also various forms of cooperation. The symbiosis of lichens (relationship between algae and fungi), corals, and their associated algae, the complex ecosystem of the human gut, and many other species are all very dependent on cooperative relationships. Organizations also exist within complex webs of cooperation and competition. You don't have to have been in business for very long to sense the truth of this. Competition is a fact of life, and sometimes comes from the most unlikely sources. But at the same time we live in an increasingly open and interlinked world, with potential partners and service providers in every area where a business leader may need help.

Energy of Enthusiasm

One of the key questions about business as a life form has to do with the energy, or life force, that powers them. What drives or enables a business to run? It is tempting to think of money as the "lifeblood" of the organization, the carrier of nutrients that provide the energy source for the business.

It's always dangerous to use metaphors, but it's not at all metaphoric to say that the energy source for your business is provided by energy spent by people in the fulfillment of its purposes. Money itself can't possibly fill that function. Money, by itself, really accomplishes nothing. A bank account does not invent things. A stock option does not fulfill a customer's requirement. What accomplishes those things? People do!

Your business runs, and remains on a healthy path, completely due to people in interaction with other people. People, interacting inside the business, or across the boundary of the business, with customers in particular, and with suppliers and others, enable your business to thrive. If customers do not spend their time thinking about and interacting with your products and services, your business will die in splendid isolation. If people do not ensure that the procurement process runs effectively, the same result will occur.

The key point here is that it's not simply energy that keeps your business at the peak of health, but *enthusiastic* energy. People who come to work fired up to make a difference. People who are willing to go the extra mile to make a customer happy. People whose minds are working overtime to make their work more effective and to keep making improvements in how their part of the business runs. People who see their work as more than just a job, but as a way to be involved in something bigger than themselves.

So where does that enthusiasm come from? Part of it, to be sure, is a result of having a great cultural alignment. Part of it is compensation and other policies that people see as fair. But a big part of this necessary enthusiasm comes straight from you, as a business leader. And this, in turn comes from the vision, passion, and persistence in the face of adversity that you display every day. The thing is, it's hard to maintain that vision, passion, and persistence in the face of business conditions that are clearly unhealthy. So, we see that a cycle is set up, which can be either a virtuous cycle of increasing enthusiasm all around or a vicious cycle of deteriorating health and energy levels.

Maturity Levels

The view that businesses are alive brings up a natural concern about where a business might be in its lifecycle at any point in time. What is healthy for a business at one stage of life might be a real health problem at a different stage of life.

Ichak Adizes provides a useful viewpoint on this issue through a number of books and his international consulting practice and educational institute (Adizes 1988). For Adizes, the difference between for-profit and not-for-profit is overrated. He claims that in the growing stages, leadership leads the people, while in the aging stages, the people lead the leadership—and they get the leadership they deserve.

On the upwardly growing side of the lifecycle, he talks about courtship, where an infatuation with the idea of a new organization infects participants, but can vanish into an inconclusive "affair." An infancy stage of a start-up organization may succumb to infant mortality or proceed to the go-go phase of success and enthusiastic growth. Later phases include adolescence, and the coveted prime phase, and then stability. The stable state can be a dangerous tipping point that may give way to an arrogant aristocracy phase, and then more or less advanced stages of bureaucracy and death.

Along the way he makes reference to disease, diagnosis, and therapy. He presages our concern with role structures and role-players by postulating key management roles of performance, administration, entrepreneuring, and integrating (PAEI). These roles are always present to greater or lesser degrees, and in different lifecycle phases exhibit varying strength and relationships with each other.

The primary message is that the growth of an enterprise goes through a predictable progression, which will make the PAEI elements predictable within ranges of behavior. Adizes does claim that it is possible to bypass some of the intermediate phases by conscious attention to the otherwise inevitable and predictable patterns.

This chapter has set the stage to understand that problems with any of these sustainment mechanisms will inevitably lead to unhealthy organizations. Concern with health-related issues will inform much of the third and fourth sections of this book. But before we get there, let's take a closer look at the way businesses and other organizations come into being as living systems, and how they continue to regenerate themselves.

CHAPTER 3

Organizations Coming to Life

This chapter takes a closer look at the process whereby organizations come to life. This establishes the groundwork for understanding how they can stay healthy, and what you can do to assure that.

People Live in Systems

One thing we know for sure is that human beings can hardly be found except within and among social groupings or organizations. The lone hermit, the feral child, the persistent recluse provide very rare exceptions that prove the rule, and are interesting exactly because of their rarity. Yet in spite of, or perhaps because of, almost total ubiquity, human organizations present tremendous challenges to our understanding. To invoke a rather well known cliché, this is like the fish who wondered, "What the heck is 'water'?" since he'd never known life outside the pond. We're so completely immersed in and among organizational affiliations that it's hard to step back and gain a clear sense of the nature of this medium in which we swim.

We also observe an interesting combination of *intentional creation* and *natural growth* of organizations. This forms a kind of hybrid of design *and* emergence. No matter how carefully an organization may be designed, it always seems that eventually it takes on a life of its own. How does this happen? What is the mechanism? And how can we gain from a deeper understanding of this mixture of intentional design and spontaneous emergence?

The difference between human organizations and all other systems, living and nonliving, comes down to these three points:

- Human organizations are consciously designed and constructed.
- Autonomous human beings join together as participants in organizations.
- Organizations themselves become autonomous, with often unexpected results.

In this chapter we will try to account for these three aspects of organizations, as a way of better understanding your business.

Definition of Life

Human organizations constitute a special class of living systems, and this has a huge impact on the business of leadership. An understanding of this impact starts with a definition of life itself. In the early 1980s Humberto Maturana and Francisco Varela, two Chilean biologists, advanced perhaps the clearest, most concise description of what it actually means to be alive. They invented the term *autopoiesis* to describe the living process of self-creation and self-maintenance. This term comes from the Greek words for "self" and "create." Autopoiesis, or self-creation, applies to biological cells and biological organisms. They wrote, "… the notion of autopoiesis is necessary and sufficient to characterize the organization of living systems." Thus, according to this viewpoint, all living systems are autopoietic and all autopoietic systems are living. Their formal definition of autopoiesis is:

> An autopoietic machine is a machine organized (defined as a unity) as a network of processes of production (transformation and destruction) of components that produces the components which: (i) through their interactions and transformations continuously regenerate and realize the network of processes (relations) that produced them; and (ii) constitute it (the machine) as a concrete unity in the space in which they (the components) exist by specifying the topological domain of its realization as such a network. (Maturana and Varela 1980)

Their definition states that a biological system continuously creates its components, while the interactions among those same components create the system itself. The system creates its parts, and the parts, in a network of processes, create the system. This is what it means to be self-creating.

It is easy to jump to the conclusion that human organizations meet this set of criteria, even though Maturana and Varela themselves were actually divided on this question. Important aspects of the human organization seem to fit nicely within this formal definition of autopoiesis, but a deeper look tells us it's not a perfect match.

Two Challenges

Comparing human organizations to biological life raises two fundamental challenges. The first challenge is the issue of the *dedication of components* to the larger entity. In the case of biological organisms, cells are fully contained, completely dedicated components of the biological entity. Likewise in the case of organizations of nonhuman species, Maturana says: "The society of bees … is an example of a third order self-referring system," where the bees are fully dedicated to the social system. But what are the components of a human organization? If we think of the component of a human organization as a *person*, we immediately see that no person is 100 percent dedicated to the higher system. Clearly cells in a body and bees in a beehive are not good models for a person in an organization. Bees don't divide their time among the hive, a job, a church, and the Rotary Club in the way people participate in multiple organizations at the same time.

The second challenge stems from the condition that autopoietic systems *create their own components*. The immediate intuitive idea that individual people are organizational components doesn't hold up to this condition either. A corporation does not *create* actual human beings. Nor does the church, the military, the government, a university, or any other human organization. The family may appear to create its components as newborn human beings, but even the family, through adoption, marriage, or other extensions does not always *create* people as its *components*.

These two challenges suggest that a complete individual human being should not be regarded as a component of a human organization. This raises the question of what does constitute the component of a business.

Nonliving Systems

As noted earlier, human organizations are consciously constructed, *and* they seem to take on lives of their own, often to the consternation of their leadership.

A term from systems science for systems that are constructed by external forces is allopoietic (François 1998). Again, the root "poiesis" denotes the concept of *making*. An allopoietic system is one that *has been made* rather than making itself. This describes a process of creation and maintenance of the system by the efforts of some external agency. It applies to manufactured products, such as automobiles and computers that are not able to continually create and refresh themselves (as much as we might wish they would!). A manufactured system (an automobile, say) does not create its own parts. Nor do the parts form relationships with each other in order to self-create the automobile.

There is a reason to consider nonliving, manufactured systems in the process of classifying organizations. Surely it is apparent that people do at least *try* to create organizations to perform certain functions, in business and elsewhere. Some people even talk about engineering an organization. At the same time, it is equally apparent that organizations are not entirely composed of nonliving, passive parts, nor can we say in any reasonable sense that they are *manufactured*. Clearly something is going on that is different from biology and also different from manufacturing. In other words, we are seeing neither autopoiesis nor allopoiesis, but a different process that is unique to human organizations.

Let's step back and ground ourselves in some additional concepts, so that we can describe more thoroughly exactly what kind of life form we see when we contemplate a business.

Learning and Imitation

As a step toward understanding the mechanisms of creation and maintenance of organizations, it's helpful to consider the notion of the meme. The meme was introduced fairly recently (Dawkins 1989) as one of two kinds of replicators that execute Charles Darwin's evolutionary algorithm. The Darwinian algorithm holds that, over time within a large population of replicators, those replicators that produce more surviving offspring leave their lines of descendents better adapted to the environment (Dennett 1995). The two kinds of replicators at work in human development and evolution, according to Dawkins, are genes and memes.

The gene is the basic unit of biological evolution, and the propagator of change and variation at the species level of organisms, including people. A successful gene is one that has three characteristics (fidelity, fecundity, and longevity) that make it successful in the competition to reproduce. Fidelity means that, for instance, a cat faithfully reproduces cats that have all the important features of a cat, and not sometimes features of a buffalo and sometimes features of a mosquito. Fecundity means that cats reproduce rapidly enough to at least exceed their death rate, and thereby continue the cat life form. Longevity means that cats live long enough, enough of the time, to actually exercise their ability to reproduce. Among the cat population, any improvement in any of these factors means that those cats that experience these improvements will be at an advantage in producing offspring that carry forward their own characteristics.

Memes, on the other hand, are ideas or behaviors, which also have the ability to replicate themselves, to change over time, and to reproduce changed forms in a kind of cultural evolution. A simple example of a meme is the song Happy Birthday, which has been handed down through generations of human beings. Another recent example of a meme is the tweet, which started a few years ago, and has spread far and wide within many human populations via the software application Twitter. Another meme is the idea of the fast-food restaurant. Another is the idea of wearing blue jeans. "Memes are replicants with the three prerequisite properties for producing an evolutionary system, replication, variance, and selection" (McNamara 2011). The successful meme, like the successful gene, is also one that has characteristics of fidelity, fecundity, and longevity, which make it successful in the competition to reproduce.

The operation of the meme derives its power from the fact that human beings, among all living species, exhibit the most pronounced propensity for imitation (Blackmore 1999). To some extent, it seems that memetic scholars have reinvented, or rediscovered, this unique ability of humans. A much earlier term for this ability was mimesis, which also refers to the human ability to try on multiple personas, literally investing ourselves in multiple roles. Plato, for instance, distinguishes between diegesis (narration and reporting) versus mimesis (imitation and representation) ("Mimesis" 2014).

Actors specialize in developing and displaying their talent for playing multiple personas. Performance and personas form the basis for the entertainment industry. And, importantly, this natural human ability also forms the basis of human organizations, as well. When a government needs an army, it creates soldiers out of raw recruits. When a society needs firemen or doctors or surveyors, it provides the incentive and the conditioning, and takes the relatively undifferentiated candidates and invests them into those roles—the performers that it needs for the challenge at hand (Butch Casanova personal communication 2015).

As a bit of an aside, the mechanism of mimesis, or of memes, at the individual level may actually arise from so-called mirror neurons.

> In the field of cognitive neuroscience, imitation is recognized as a fundamental human skill. Neurons have been identified which match action perception with action execution.... The mirror neuron system (MNS) appears to be the biological motor component permitting ... 'mimetic skill' required for the evolution of culture and cognition. (McNamara 2011)

Commitments, and Agreements

With this background, a general pattern of organizational behavior can be understood with the help of a particular class of memes, which predisposes people to make commitments to organizations, to increase their participation over time, and for their participation to attract other people to make similar commitments. This very pervasive process draws strongly upon the natural tendency for people to imitate each other's behavior, as discussed above. As people participate in organizations they have an opportunity to observe and mimic behaviors that exemplify and support those organizations.

The replicating power of commitments increases as they become externalized in the form of verbal or recorded agreements. A simple agreement might be when a person asks a stranger for a favor and the other person agrees to do so. Or the eye contact and subtle movement of head or hand that lets another motorist merge in traffic. More elaborate and permanent examples include terms and conditions of business contracts and clauses in laws and regulations. There are special kinds of formative agreements, such as charters, constitutions, and by-laws, which declare the very existence and initial commitments of an organization. Textual and electronic representations of agreements provide both fidelity and longevity—key characteristics of successful replicators, as we've seen.

Once an agreement has become incorporated into a person's thoughts and behavior, it increases its survival potential to the extent that it does two things: (1) expands the set of related commitments made by the person to the organization, so as to dominate more of the person's attention; and (2) stimulates the person to behave in such a way as to bring additional parties into similar commitments to the organization.

Federated Autonomous Systems

We have seen that some types of systems *emerge and grow*, while other types of systems are *designed and manufactured*. Some systems are alive, and others are not. Living systems include cells, organs, and organisms. Designed and manufactured systems include machines, buildings, and software.

We have also seen that human beings have a special ability to learn from each other, in a form of mimicry, which may be hard-wired in the form of mirror neurons, and is also formalized into contractual and other agreements. Human organizations (unlike bee hives, ant colonies, wolf packs, whale pods, and slime molds) are both living *and* designed. However, the conscious design of human organizations is a matter of degree and is often quite limited, or even elusive. Participants in human organizations have a high degree of autonomy, such that it's not possible to focus their full and undivided attention on a single group to the exclusion of all others. So the organization reaches a level of autonomy through the joining together (a federation) of people, who, at the same time, retain much of their own autonomy, even though joined together.

Figure 3.1 summarizes this discussion, by showing three levels of living systems side by side, including their identities as concrete unities,

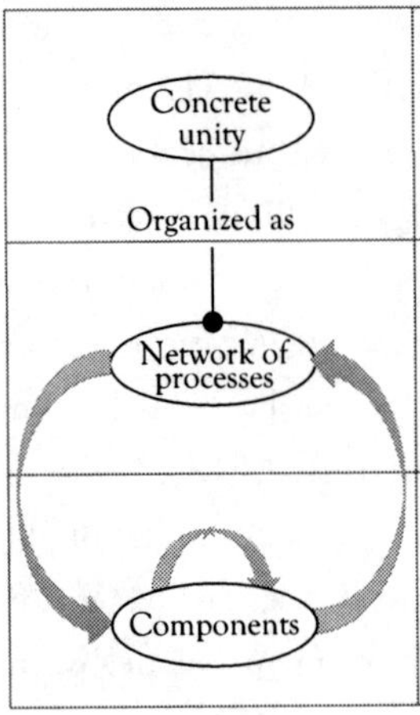

Concrete unity / Organized as	Cell	Person	Organization
Network of processes	Metabolism Protein synthesis Replication etc.	Circulation Immunity Cognition etc.	Recruit Train Deploy etc.
Components	Membrane Cytoskeleton Organelles etc.	Cells Organs Skeleton etc.	Offerings Services Roles Role-players etc.

Figure 3.1 Levels of life

their organizing networks of processes, and their components that create and are created by their processes. This summary makes it clear that organizations actually do emerge and sustain themselves as a form of life. This process can be resisted or embraced by leaders of organizations, with major consequences for their success.

CHAPTER 4

Maintaining Stable Viability

This chapter expands upon a key concept introduced in the comparison between biological and organizational life. We mentioned the ability to manage variety and to maintain stability amidst various flows. In order for your business to remain viable (capable of life) it must be able to call upon controlling services that provide requisite variety, a concept introduced by Ross Ashby, a leading pioneer in the field of cybernetics (Ashby 1956). You can think of a variety in terms of disturbances, unexpected occurrences, and just plain noise and complications of doing business. In order to keep these disturbances at a level where they don't destroy your business, controlling mechanisms need to have as many responses as the factors you need to control.

It's probably fair to say that the best-known application of the concept of viability based on controlling variety within organizations can be found in Stafford Beer's notion of the viable systems model (VSM). Beer invented the field of *management* cybernetics to apply control theory to organizations, such as the steel manufacturing plants where he worked as a manager early in his career (Beer 1985).

Homeostasis

A good example of a control mechanism in the mechanical world is the simple thermostat. The purpose of a thermostat is to regulate the temperature in a space. It works through a temperature sensing function, a rule for an acceptable temperature range, and the ability to activate heating and cooling units. These operate together to maintain the temperature of a room at a comfortable level.

All such control units can be grouped under the term homeostat, and their effects under the term homeostasis. Their general purpose is to hold certain conditions as steady as possible, under conditions of assault by particular forces. Homeostasis applies to mechanical situations, such as the thermostat and heating and cooling devices, but it also applies to biological life forms, such as human beings. The endocrine glands are examples of biological homeostats. They create compounds to regulate various bodily functions. For instance, the pineal gland produces melatonin that helps regulate sleep.

The VSM provides a way of expressing the function of homeostasis in organizations. Obviously, buildings and biological bodies are physical, and subject to physical forces that need to be managed. Organizations, on the other hand, are actually invisible and intangible entities, but which are also subject to forces that need to be controlled. In a way similar to how we try to keep our homes at a nice comfortable temperature, in your business you're looking to maintain a minimum of drama. You want to reduce crisis and firefighting situations to a minimum. You're trying to detect disturbances early and to deal with them while they're still small. You're trying to avoid situations where management overreacts to a threat, and then overreacts to the reverse threat caused by the overshoot, and then overreacts to ... well, you get the picture!

Beer borrowed a couple of terms from engineering (attenuation and amplification) to talk about homeostasis. Attenuation is like a filter that reduces a flow across some boundary. Amplification, as we know, provides the reverse function; increasing the impact of, say, a note played by a guitar at a rock concert. In the case of managing an organization, the flows we are talking about in management cybernetics are information flows. There are dynamic stability points we desire, where meaningful information gets through to where it can be acted upon, while avoiding an overwhelming overload.

Figure 4.1 provides an abstract view of a stability mechanism, where the endless potential input is received, translated, and filtered for relevance before being processed into new ideas and intentions to act. The intentional responses are then aimed at a portion of the marketplace, translated into understandable and compelling terms, and amplified to a level that competes with all the noise out there.

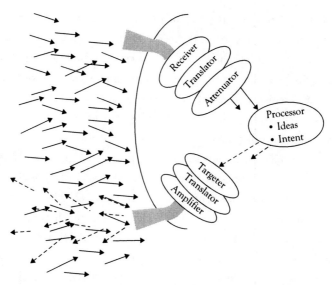

Figure 4.1 Enterprise homeostat

Stability Regulators Everywhere

Your business has many places where such regulators help maintain its health. Clearly at those places where there is direct interaction with the market, in the form of clients, potential clients, suppliers, and so on, the operational parts of the business want to receive important market signals, without being overwhelmed by irrelevant background noise and distraction. This is an attenuation function. At the same time, you want an amplifier that is able to get your own message across, in a way that attracts those you want to do business with, and that penetrates *their* attenuation mechanisms (gatekeepers, etc.).

Internal attenuation points summarize and otherwise filter the massive flow of raw transactions, as reports from the operational units feed into higher levels of management and decision-making. At the same time, those higher levels of management need to amplify instructions, changes of plan, and so on, in order to get the attention of the operational units. You can start to see the structure that is being portrayed here, of services being performed for external and internal role-players, accompanied by information. Erring on the side of too much information *or* too little information can each damage the health of your business.

We also recognize that a lot of interaction exists among operational units themselves. There is often a need to coordinate shared resources, and make sure consistent messages are being broadcast to the marketplace. Actions taken by one unit often stimulate a reaction in another unit, which can set up disruptive and damaging oscillations in the organization. An example of damping the oscillation among units might be found in a university, where faculty members maintain a schedule of classroom usage so that they do not continually bump into each other in trying to use the same rooms at the same times. Beer points out that this is something that can be worked out close to the action, rather than by upper management dictate. In fact, much of what promotes health in a business is the idea of subsidiarity—the practice of allowing decision-making and coordination to occur at the lowest level where it can be done effectively.

We can think of attenuator or amplifier homeostats that support healthy delegation (subsidiarity). For example, at a customer-facing interaction point on the edge of the business, tools include attenuation of noise, but also amplification of signals from the client that may be faint, but that make a difference. Not just feedback cards, but what they are actually *saying* verbally and even body language. And looking in the reverse direction, the outward-bound communication can amplify messages that convey client-specific concerns, and attenuate up-sale messages when the amplified messages from clients indicate they are not receptive.

Recursive Viability

Any system of interest can always be seen as a subsystem of some higher-level system, which in turn exists as a subsystem within a system at a still higher level. Systems thinkers often follow a rule of thumb of identifying the system to focus attention on, and then understand it in terms of the higher-level system it is part of, and the subsystems that it contains. Organizations can thus be seen as fractal, or recursive, as a result of these various levels of systems embedded within systems. A lot of complexity can be understood by recognizing multiple such dimensions of recursion. For instance a university that is embedded in a state university system, inside a national education system, on the one hand, may also be embedded in a university town, embedded in a county, embedded in a state.

From this discussion we get an inkling about how this viewpoint provides powerful diagnostic tools. However, before we get there, let's take a look at how the simple acts of service between people are the building blocks of the basic mechanism of human organization.

PART II

The Living Web of Services

CHAPTER 5

All Services, All the Time

As we have seen, the basic process of creation, sustainment, and evolution of human organizations mirrors similar processes in biological life. Now, in this chapter, we're going to look at a counterpart concept, which goes hand in hand with agreements and commitments to create a more complete picture of how the life of a business is created and sustained.

I hope you can at least momentarily entertain the notion that every business may usefully be seen as a service business, and even what we normally think of as products can be viewed according to the services they provide. This is the essence of the "all-services, all-the-time" perspective. This perspective stems directly from the observation that people, with their talent, knowledge, skills, and experience constitute the ultimate source of value. No matter what business you're in, this perspective can serve you well.

19th Century Wisdom

The all-services, all-the-time viewpoint has strong underpinning in the work of Frédéric Bastiat, a French statesman and economist of the 19th Century. In his day, Bastiat was a tireless advocate for free trade, and he made a witty and entertaining case against the regressive effects of tariffs and other barriers to exchange (Bastiat 2011).

The most fundamental pattern within Bastiat's political economy consists of (1) desires and wants, (2) efforts, and (3) satisfaction of desires. *Desires* inspire *efforts* to achieve *satisfactions*. His list of human desires and wants includes (in general order of urgency): respiration, food, clothing, lodging, preservation or re-establishment of health, locomotion, security, instruction, diversion, and sense of the beautiful. He defines labor as the *effort* to satisfy desires, and it may be physical, intellectual, or even moral.

Bastiat talks about the "indefinite expansibility" of the desires and wants of people. Not infinite, but indefinite, so that as certain wants are satisfied, others come into view. He separates the ideas of wealth and value, saying that wealth is to be found in utility, which is the combination of the gifts of nature and of human labor, while *value* is the result of the effort of a person on behalf of others, and must be recompensed.

He gives examples of water, air, and energy to emphasize the point that, when these are freely available to all, there is no basis for putting value on them, and therefore no basis for exchange.

> If we all always had a spring right at our feet, evidently water would not have any value, since there would be no occasion to exchange it. But if it is half a mile away, we must go and get it; that is work, and there is the origin of its value. If it is a mile away, that is double work, and hence double value, although the utility remains the same. [If] I go and get [water] myself, I render myself a service by taking some pains. If I entrust this task to another, I put him to some trouble and owe him a service…. Air is a gratuitous gift of Nature; it has no value…. But if you enter a diving bell and have a man send down air to you with a pump for two hours, he will be put to some trouble; he will render you a service; you will have to repay him. Will you pay for the air? No, for the labor…. Services are exchanged for services…. *Do this for me, and I will do that for you.* It is very trivial, very commonplace; it is, nonetheless, the beginning, the middle, and the end of economic science …. By the general law of service for service, the receivers of current services must recompense the efforts that have been made for them.

Chains of Services

But, wait, I hear you say. What about services that are simply paid for? And of course, the normal case *is* that services are simply paid for with money. But here's Bastiat on that point.

The primitive form of exchange is barter which has … two wants as the motivating force, two efforts as the means, two satisfactions as the result.… Barter cannot go beyond a small circle of persons acquainted with one another. Humanity would soon have reached the limits of the division of labor, the limits of progress, if a means of facilitating exchange had not been found.… When this type of intermediate commodity is resorted to, two economic phenomena appear, which are called sale and purchase.… Exchange is not complete until the [person] who has made an effort for another [person] receives in return an equivalent service, that is, a satisfaction.

We thus sell services for an "intermediate commodity" (some form of money) and then eventually buy equivalent services.

Some efforts are directed toward services currently being delivered, while other efforts make it possible to deliver services in the future. Bastiat gives us the example of the water carrier, who makes his own barrow and cask and then amortizes that effort across the many actual services of providing water. In agriculture he talks about plowing, sowing, harrowing, weeding, harvesting, on the one hand versus clearing, enclosing, draining, and improving the land, on the other.

Bastiat summarizes the cumulative effect of services compounded across a whole economy, resulting in a powerful concatenation of effort. Remember, this is from a mid-19th Century point of view, but it's easy to transfer this thinking to the 21st Century, where the networks and forces are vastly more powerful. As Bastiat reports, a common worker purchases a pair of cotton stockings for half day of wages. This is nothing compared to the effort that it would take for him to perform every aspect of bringing those stockings into existence. His small price (multiplied by all buyers of stockings and other cotton goods) provides recompense for the chain of labor, and the interest on capital that enlisted the gratuitous services of nature. That is, "Capital does not consist of the vegetative force that has made cotton germinate and flower, but in the pains taken by the planter." And we might add the weaver, the transportation network, the marketing and sales service, and so on.

Back to the Future

More recently (much more recently!), two professors of marketing, Stephen Vargo and Robert Lusch made the case for a service-dominant perspective on commercial activity. They contrast service-dominant logic with the prevailing view in the 20th century:

> The old dominant logic: The purpose of economic activity is to make and distribute things that can be sold. To be sold, these things must be embedded with utility and value during the production and distribution processes and must offer to the consumer superior value in relation to competitors' offerings. The firm should set all decision variables at a level that enables it to maximize the profits from the sale of output. For both maximum production control and efficiency, the good should be standard-ized and produced away from the market. The good can then be inventoried until demanded and then delivered to the consumer at a profit. (Lusch and Vargo 2005)

This seems to indicate that services-orientation is a matter of perspec-tive, with the pendulum of perception recently swinging strongly back toward Bastiat's position that exchange of services, mediated by some *intermediate commodity* (money of some kind) forms the basis for all economic activity. That perspective creates the opportunity to bring the services aspect into the foreground. For instance, the painter of a chassis in an automobile manufacturing plant can be classified as a service pro-vider. That is true if the painters are subcontracting to the manufacturer, but how is it really different if they are employees performing the service of painting? IBM Research can be seen as a service provider within IBM as a computer manufacturer and software vendor. Whole industries, such as the consumer electronics industry, have been broken down into multi-ple enterprises that provide specialized services to each other in complex supply networks.

One of the ways this dynamic is playing out in education and the workplace is through programs like Services Science, Management,

Engineering and Design, whereby service-thinking is introduced in programs of study for the next generations of business leaders (Spohrer and Kwan 2009).

Products Offer Services

From the all-services, all-the-time perspective, even those things we typically call "products" can be seen as services, as well. Bastiat talked about the service provided by a person pumping air to another person working underwater. Today we can update that by pointing to a SCUBA outfit that provides air to a person who is underwater. The SCUBA outfit, designed and manufactured, provides a similar service, and therefore also has value, for the same reason.

Manufactured products are all intended to perform services for buyers. It's just that in the product case, the service is released from constraints of time and distance. The manufacturer does not have to be present at the same time and location as the recipient of the service, and the service in many cases can be performed over and over for weeks, months, or years into the future, without further interaction with the manufacturer. In these cases the co-creation of value happens in stages: the manufacturing stage and the usage stage. A car exists to provide a transportation service, but without direct intervention of the original maker of the car. With a services mindset, automakers have taken advantage of the electronics on board many modern cars, to offer maintenance and guidance services that go beyond simple transportation. But the transportation itself is clearly a service, performed remotely in time and location. A chair exists to provide the service of a place to sit. A flashlight exists to provide the service of a portable light source.

An interesting exercise is to try to think of some product for which this relationship does not hold true. This exercise is left to the imagination of the reader!

Another way to look at this is from the "jobs-to-be-done" perspective. This way of thinking was laid out in *The Innovator's Solution*, which talks about "hiring" a product to perform a job that needs to be done in the life of a customer. An interesting example is the morning milkshake.

A surprising profile emerged from a fast-food restaurant, where researchers found that a high percentage of milkshakes were purchased in the early morning. They found that the job that morning commuters needed to be done consisted of a combination of (1) reducing the boredom of a long commute, (2) consuming nutrition that would last well into the morning, and (3) being easy and hassle-free to consume. These commuters "hired" a milkshake to perform a "job" that needed to be done. In short, milkshake as a service! (Christensen 2003).

Services Systems Protocol

At a relatively high level (say enterprise to enterprise) there has been important work on service systems or service entities, including nested networks of service entities. An interesting protocol has been proposed as a way of understanding the way service systems work together to co-create valuable outcomes for both providers and recipients. Figure 5.1 lays out a model of service value co-creation that follows various paths through Interact-Serve-Propose-Agree-Realize (ISPAR) episodes. This model covers basic interaction decision points between systems, which may lead to one of several potential outcomes.

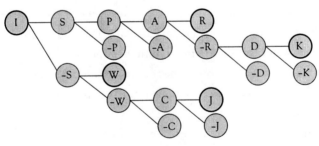

Figure 5.1 Paths through service interaction episodes

Note: I = Interaction; S = Service interaction; P = Proposal communicated; −P = Proposal not communicated; A = Agreement reached; −A = Agreement not reached; R = Realized value co-creation; −R = Not realized value co-creation; D = Dispute; −D = Nondispute; K = OK resolution for all interested parties; −K = Not OK resolution for all interested parties; −S = Nonservice interaction; W = Welcome nonservice interaction; −W = Unwelcome nonservice interaction; C = Criminal interaction; −C = Noncriminal interaction; J = Justice realized; −J = Justice not realized

An interaction episode is a series of activities jointly undertaken by two service systems. Broadly speaking, interactions can be service interactions (interactions that aim to co-create value) or non-service interactions. For an interaction to be a service interaction, a proposal must be made by one party to another, agreement must be reached between the parties, and value must be realized by both. If value is not realized, there may be a dispute, which in turn may or may not be resolved to the satisfaction of both parties. [An] interaction ... may be welcome or unwelcome, and some unwelcome interactions may be illegal interactions. (Maglio et al. 2009)

As we expand the scope of what services entail, many more instances of work and interaction are included. For instance, it does not require a specific proposal to be made in every case for an interaction to provide a service. However, it is true that instances of casual interaction, where neither party realizes any form of value, might be excluded from our definition. This is another of those places where I'll leave it to you to think about interactions that are totally neutral. At the same time, it's easy to think about interactions that might be unwelcome, or even criminal, so that the protocol in Figure 5.1 would apply.

Where This Takes You

We are talking about services in a more general way than the enterprise-to-enterprise service systems that the ISPAR model supports. We are also going *far* beyond the formal definitions of services and service businesses as used by international trade associations and government agencies to quantify product versus service components of the GDP.

The all-services, all-the-time perspective makes it clear that no matter your business, you offer services, sometimes interactively; sometimes with deferred time horizons; sometimes when the customer is present at your location; and sometimes when the customer is halfway around the world. Once you start to see all businesses as in the business of service, all work as performing services of some kind, and all products existing to provide services at a distance in time and space, a kind of pattern language starts to become useful. The kinds of questions that are prompted by taking an all-services perspective include:

- Who receives the value that the service provides?
- What purpose is this interactive or deferred service intended to satisfy?
- What desire, want, or need does it fulfill?
- What value is being created for the receiver?
- How effective is it?
- Are we being properly rewarded based on effective performance?
- Who decides what level of value requires a certain level of remuneration?
- How else might the receiver's desire be fulfilled?
- What potential providers of alternate services might become competitors?

In other words, the services perspective is based on a recipient with reactions and judgments that you really need to listen to. In turn, careful listening opens up vistas of service enhancements and follow-on opportunities to establish on-going relationships.

The early 21st century provides a particularly appropriate opportunity to emphasize this focus on services, just as the Internet of Things is starting to gain momentum and new generations of people who have never experienced the world without powerful computers and communication devices in their pockets are coming into the workforce. It's easier now than ever before to see all business as a web or graph of interconnected services. Or, as we've heard from Bastiat: "Services are exchanged for services. ... *Do this for me, and I will do that for you.* It is very trivial, very commonplace; it is, nonetheless, the beginning, the middle, and the end of economic science."

CHAPTER 6

Service-Role Structures

In previous chapters we have discussed the dream of business owner-ship, and its daunting difficulties in practice, based on large numbers of moving parts and organizations with minds of their own. We have con-fronted the problem of how organizations create the components that in turn create organizations as webs of commitments to provide services. We have seen how the services perspective helps explain how this all works to create and capture value. Now let's look more deeply into the actual com-ponents of organizations, service-roles that embody this federating power of commitment, and harness it in value-creating services.

Roles as Building Blocks

A straightforward, 50-year-old, statement on the importance of role as building blocks for organizations can be found here: "An organization might almost be defined as a structure of roles tied together with lines of communication. The cellular units of organization are not men, but, as it were, parts of men, men acting in a certain role" (Boulding 1956). Aside from the dated-sounding use of the masculine pronoun, this quote leads us in the right direction. In following that direction, let's take a look at definitions of roles, role-players, and role-nets, represented as service-graphs (Mike McClintock personal communication 2015) as the component structure of service-providing organizations.

Well-known roles include customer, employee, regulator, sales or distribution channel, and supplier, as well as more general types such as performers, managers, and recipients of various types of results. Here we want to explore more deeply the roles that you as a business leader need and hope to be performed within your organization. These are the roles that define the abilities and the performances that produce results within and beyond the borders of your business. These are roles that provide the structure to understand the myriad services performed by everyone who participates in your business (including yourself).

The underlying energy behind the structure of service-roles, and the endless process of federation of autonomies, stems from the motives of desires, needs, and wants that we have already seen in Bastiat's list: respiration, food, clothing, lodging, preservation or re-establishment of health, locomotion, security, instruction, diversion, and a sense of the beautiful. We see another manifestation of this kind of human energy in Abraham Maslow's hierarchy of physiological needs, safety needs, need for love and belonging, and need for esteem and for self-actualization ("Maslow" 2015).

What we see here is the interface between the biological and psychological person and the person as federated into the service-role structure of the organization. This is similar to the interface between physics and chemistry, and the interface between chemistry and biology. It is very important for leaders of organizations to realize and account for these human psychological dimensions as the basis for the service-role structures of their organizations.

Service-Roles

For our purposes the term *service-role* simply means the definition of a role that a person can agree to assume, and that is based on an agreement to perform and provide certain services in an organization. When Boulding talks about a "structure of roles," such a structure needs to start with an understanding of the roles themselves.

A service relationship of any kind between one person and other people forms the basis of the definition of a service-role. We have talked about these relationships in terms of how they form federations among autonomous entities, giving rise to separately autonomous organizations. As we saw, the memetic tendency to make commitments to organizations lies at the heart of all these structures. A service-role definition carries a set of responsibilities for delivering results through the performance of services. Performances are based on abilities and other characteristics that match with potential role-players who possess those characteristics.

A service-role definition may be explicit, (e.g., contained in a written job description) but may also contain implicit or tacit expectations. In many cases the service-role definition is entirely tacit, and only discovered through experience in practice. The service-role definition may evolve over time in response to evolving situations. Such evolution involves the co-creation of expectations and performance by serving and receiving role-players.

Role-Players

The term role-player simply denotes a person who is committed to, or held to account, based on the expectations defined by a service-role definition. Role-players are differentiated broadly into those who *provide* services and the recipients, who *receive* services.

Often the term role-player refers to a person who devotes some amount of time to fulfilling the service-role expectations. At the same time, it is not unusual to see this term used in connection with an organization, on the one hand, or some technological mechanism (e.g., a software application) on the other hand. These usages point toward a fractal pattern that applies at different levels of the organization.

Role-Nets

Service-roles naturally become attracted into complexes of commitments that bind people together in purposeful ways. These role-nets exhibit patterns that constitute a pervasive architectural dimension of human organizations. Role-nets can proliferate to arbitrary levels of complexity, as one role-net becomes integrated with other role-nets. In other words, a role-net is itself a network of related service-roles and role-nets, which seeks to replicate itself in cooperation with, or in competition against, other role-nets.

A role-net generally forms around a focal point of interest in some thing or class of things in the world. For instance, a role-net may form around a certain part or assembly used by a manufacturer, which involves design, engineering, and shop floor role-players. A sports team constitutes a role-net that forms around a shared desire to participate in a particular sport, joining together the manager and coach roles, equipment handling role, and the athlete roles themselves.

The foundation of any role-net is some human motivation, which can be a survival mechanism, coercion, pursuit of pleasure, and so on. Shared motivation forms the basis for role-nets, and nested networks of role-nets. Role-nets compete with each other for mindshare of their human participants. Each of us only has finite time, so there are limits to the set of time demands that can be sustained by any individual person, and therefore the numbers of roles and role-nets we can effectively participate in.

Successful role-nets, as organizational replicators, have the ability to stay relatively constant (fidelity), are relatively easily adopted by others (fecundity), and have the staying power to maintain the energy level of participation (longevity).

As role-nets, and nested networks of role-nets, become more elaborate, involving common commitments held by increasing numbers of people, they eventually pass a threshold where they become full-fledged organizations, capable of sustaining themselves over extended periods of time. This threshold is passed when the organization gains a certain level of autonomy, formed by the relationships among participating role-nets, which it continuously creates. Interestingly, this is somewhat independent of any founding or chartering documents involved.

Role-nets, as components of a human organization, have the ability to spawn endless numbers of additional role-nets. These new components may remain part of the original human organization, or may spin off and become autonomous in their own right. In this way, an organization is not only self-creating, but also reproductive. Reproducing an organization is often quite conscious, involving founding documents, franchise agreements, and so on. In this way we see the interplay between design and emergence in organizations.

Figure 6.1 displays a snippet of a role-net, focused on a kind of X-ray of a service-role. Here we see a generic service-role, magnified. This visualization supports the notion of co-creation of value by the interaction of a providing party and a receiving party. In addition, we see that this figure illustrates the notion of give-and-take, performance and reward (on both sides of the interaction). As Lusch and Vargo put it, "actors in

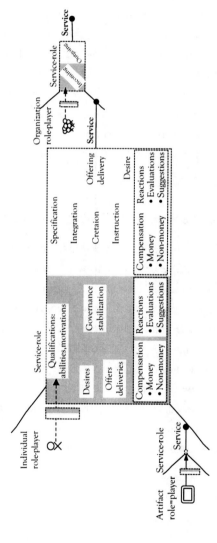

Figure 6.1 Network of service-roles

an exchange are both service providers and service beneficiaries" (Lusch and Vargo 2014).

The particular role in focus shows one primary player, in this case an individual person who matches the qualifications in terms of abilities and motivations needed. We see that there is an input and an output side of the service-role rectangle, with the main focus on the service itself, connected to a counterpart recipient service-role, which in this case is being played by an organizational role-player. The individual role-player is assisted by some kind of artifact (lower left), which is fulfilling a service-role that supports the role in focus. So, we can see a network is forming, with three service-roles, each with input and output aspects, each with qualifications, governance, needs or requirements, each making and receiving offers and services, and each making and receiving compensation and feedback.

Information Technology Playing Service-Roles

Since we mentioned a service-role being played by an artifact in relation to Figure 6.1, it makes sense to follow up with some specific thoughts about artifacts as role-players in service-roles. Earlier we made the case that everything we call products actually exist to provide a special class of service, where the provider and the recipient co-create value, even when separated by time and space. Again, this is not the official government view of services for tax and recording purposes, but it is the mindset that we bring to all types of work, as the source of all value creation.

In that context, an even *more* special class of products that provide services remotely in terms of time and distance consists of products (hardware and software) that we generally think of in terms of information technology (IT).

Services Offered by Technology

The main reason organizations invest in information technology is because of the services it provides. The fundamental service, of course, is the capture and recording of information about the business, and making that information available instantly, remotely, and in various forms and summaries. IT helps integrate events that have common properties (a policy, a coverage, a bill, a claim by the same person, or a series of inter-actions between a citizen and a town government, etc.) Let's not forget the services offered by technology in getting the word out to our consti-tuencies, fostering business relationships, and acting as general amplifiers of our messages to the world.

Specifically, in the cases of services for customers of the business, we're really in the age of services actually being offered via technology. "Global-mobile-social (Glo-Mo-So) platforms enable service producers to combine three elements: integration via the global communications platform, universal delivery via mobile devices, and collaboration across service systems via social business software" (Hastings and Saperstein 2014).

On the other hand, while IT may be a *provider* of services, IT does not *create* services. Rather the technology itself is a form of prosthesis that enhances the ability of the role-players who create and deliver service offerings. The technology is no more living than an artificial limb used by a person. But technologies and tools clearly have major impact on achiev-ing the results of services. Where, then, is accountability when technology performs services formerly performed by human beings, or introduces functional capability that was not even possible before? Mechanisms do not have responsibility for their own actions. When technology is increas-ingly inserted into our business interactions, there is a set of accountabil-ities that includes creators, installers, and maintainers of the technology. This accountability linkage is not always understood as explicit responsi-bilities, and can therefore become a dangerous point of potential abdica-tion of responsibility (McDavid 2012).

Services Supported by Technology

Where services touch the customer, there are seemingly infinite ways that service-roles can be supported. Think about how it would be in the check-in areas at airports if there were no kiosks, and every passenger had to be checked-in by agents who had no terminals to access online records. Think about when the power goes down in the supermarket and bar-code scanners cease to operate at the point of sale.

The important trend, which makes so much difference in the world of services, is the increasing ability to offer more and more services anywhere in the world, at any time. This is obviously a function of the Internet, and various forms of web-enabled information technologies. At the moment it seems that more and more people are abandoning the notion of IT in favor of a focus on "digital." On one level, digital just means computers are involved. But somewhere along the line there seems to have been a rebirth of the notion of digital transformation of business. Chief Digital Officers (CDOs) started popping up. These CDOs tend to deal with, and sometimes compete with, Chief Marketing Officers. This doesn't change the fact that we have more and more technology supporting all facets of promoting and delivering services, and once again the issue of accountability arises.

Constraints Offered by Technology

Perhaps that wording sounds a little odd, but I really *mean* "offered by." Constraints offered by technology are two-fold. On the one hand, technology may be offering constraints that serve the purpose of healthy attenuation. This is the slightly unexpected way of thinking about constraints. In my observation, this feature of technology is underappreciated, largely because neither business-people, nor IT experts, tend to consciously think in terms of homeostasis, attenuation, or information filters. However, we did cover homeostasis earlier in our section on organizational cybernetics. We showed that this is actually a very important aspect of keeping businesses healthy.

Every time an application has a controlling format for a particular field, or some kind of validity check, this is a healthy constraint in the form of IT attenuation. If an address already knows the ZIP code before you type it, or if an application guesses your e-mail based on the first character you type, you save a bit of time, which all adds up. There are much more significant attenuations in the areas of security, privacy, accuracy, and enforcement of myriad business rules. Conscious consideration of IT applications as suppliers of attenuating and amplifying services provides powerful design rules for IT.

On the other hand, IT applications may be designed so as to preclude features of the services that *could be* offered. Are we capturing all the characteristics of customers that would be helpful in our interactions with them? Do we have the reporting features that make the best use of the data we've already captured? If the answer is "No" to such question, the technology we're currently using may be getting in the way of important functions of the business. Why do these blockages occur? Maybe it's programmer convenience. Or, maybe simpler technology really *is* better. Maybe more functionality would actually be confusing or unnecessarily time-consuming. It's often very useful to ask why these design decisions have been made in IT artifacts and to get a bit pushy about getting answers. It could be a matter of business health to determine how well or badly the business is served by its information systems.

Services Required by Technology

Now, here's the real rub. Technologies of all kinds, including informational and digital technologies, require a whole host of services themselves. Assembly line and robotics technologies require maintenance and set-up services. Just within IT, set-up maintenance, integration, and rationalization, data capture, data cleansing are ravenous consumers of services.

In particular, we need to consider the consultants and trainers who bring tools to organize the interface between your business and your information technology. These are the providers who specialize in such approaches as COBIT, ITIL, TOGAF, and so on. They also can be seen as fitting into the category of lifting burdens from leadership, by providing a special case of "writing things down" as we'll see. Here are brief definitions of these methods and their associated tools. This is very much a tip of an iceberg:

COBIT

COBIT 5 is the only business framework for the governance and management of enterprise IT. It is the product of a global task force and development team from ISACA, a nonprofit, independent association of nearly 100,000 governance, security, risk and assurance professionals in 160 countries.

COBIT stands for Control Objectives for Information and Related Technology. ISACA stands for Information Systems Audit and Control Association (COBIT 2015).

TOGAF

> The Open Group Architecture Framework (TOGAF) is a
> framework for IT architecture which provides an approach for
> designing, planning, implementing, and governing an enterprise
> information technology architecture ... TOGAF is a high level
> approach to design. It is typically modeled at four levels: Business,
> Application, Data, and Technology. It relies heavily on modular-
> ization, standardization, and already existing, proven technologies
> and products. ("TOGAF" 2015)

ITIL

"ITIL, formerly known as the Information Technology Infrastructure
Library, is a set of practices for IT service management (ITSM) that
focuses on aligning IT services with the needs of business."

ITIL is structured as five volumes:

- Service Strategy: understands organizational objectives and
  customer needs.
- Service Design: turns the service strategy into a plan for
  delivering the business objectives.
- Service Transition: develops and improves capabilities for
  introducing new services into supported environments.
- Service Operation: manages services in supported
  environments.
- Continual Service Improvement: achieves services incremental
  and large-scale improvements ("ITIL" 2015).

Note the emphasis on *services* throughout the ITIL structure of strategy, design, transition, operation, and improvement.

Service-roles, role-players, and networks of roles can be viewed as the
fundamental mechanism for creating ever-more elaborate organizations.
It turns out that a surprising variety of characteristics come into play
when we look deeply into roles themselves. That's what the next chapter
examines—the variety of factors for matching roles to the players of roles.

CHAPTER 7

Characteristics of Service-Roles

In the last chapter we explored a fundamental structure of organizations in terms of structures of service-roles, role-players, and role-nets, represented as service-graphs. Here we focus on an exploration of how these structures take on variations and attributes in the context of actual organizations, like your business. You should already be seeing practical applications of these structures and patterns as you think about the design and the health of your business.

Figure 7.1 provides a kind of graphic overview for the generic pattern that we explore in this chapter. In this depiction, the service-role has been split into the provider and recipient aspects, to emphasize the transactional nature of services, but this shouldn't override the combined reality of these aspects that we saw in Figure 6.1.

Role-Players

Service-role structures only give rise to organizations, including businesses, when there are humans and artifacts that actually play those service-roles. We need to understand the provider and recipient side of symmetrical service relationships.

- Provider—A provider may be a paid role-player (e.g., employee or contractor), a very common form of provider. All organizations may also have voluntary role-players. In the case of prisons, public schools, and so on, there are also people in the position of involuntary role-players, though this is not a major focus for us in this book.

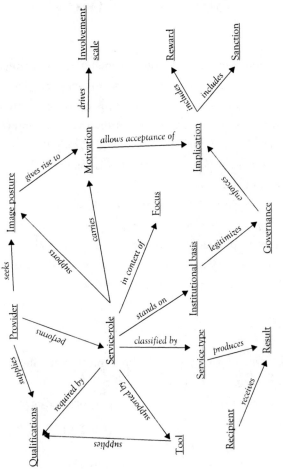

Figure 7.1 Service-role aspects

- Recipients—Some recipients receive the results from a
  provider in a value coproduction relationship, while other
  recipients receive payments or other responses (complaints
  and compliments, reviews, etc.) from the first kind of
  recipient. It is also true that much of the activity of any
  organization is expended in the performance of internal
  services that aggregate to common goals.

As we've also seen, not only are there reciprocal providers and recipients on the two sides of a service but also that every service-role itself has an input and output side.

Qualifications

In any consideration of service-roles, we need to think about qualifications, which we see in both Figures 6.1 and 7.1. Below is a list of various kinds of qualifications that come into play in various conditions:

- Natural ability—In general, we tend to think about
  qualifications in terms of the *ability* of a role-player to
  perform the services implied or specified by the service-role
  structure. However, not all qualifications for playing in a
  service-role are simply based on natural abilities alone.
- Experience—Often the qualification to play a service-role is
  specified in terms of experience in already playing that role
  somewhere else, or some other role that is similar enough so
  that the learning curve will not be too arduous.
- Training—The primary route, beyond experience, to become
  qualified to play various service-roles is through education or
  training. This may include specialized forms of knowledge
  transmission, such as coaching, tutoring, and mentoring.
- Certification—Often it is not enough to have experience or
  learn from others. For many service-roles it is necessary to
  produce a certificate of some kind, which provides tangible
  evidence of qualification for playing the role.

- Connections—To be realistic, it's important to note that a common qualification is expressed as, as the old saying goes, "It's not what you know, but who you know." Qualification through connections is a fact of life, as frustrating as that might be, which may be something to consider in the diagnosis of healthy and unhealthy situations.
- Birthright—An extension of non-knowledge-based service-role qualification can occur when service-roles are defined through tribal or traditional authority. This is the case of literally being born into a role, such as first son, or member of a royal family. This is also a common situation in family owned businesses, where unhealthy situations often arise as a result.

Institutional Basis

Underlying the ability to offer and perform various services is the institutional basis that permits or mandates the creation of those service-roles and service-role structures in the first place. Here are a few of the institutional forms that can spawn service-roles:

- Employment—The employment roles constitute one of the most common and widely recognized examples of the concept of roles. Everyone recognizes the existence of the service-role definition of a job. Depending on that actual service-role definition, which typically involves a "job description," the roles are specified, and role-nets in terms of who works together are generally specified as well.
- Ownership—A set of service-roles cluster around the role of business ownership, with responsibilities to the business itself, clients, suppliers, and community. This kind of role forms the basis for a role-net as well, as soon as there is an ownership group beyond a single owner–founder or sole trader (solopreneur).
- Stewardship—A stewardship service-role structure requires a kind of solicitous accountability toward the asset being

stewarded. A park ranger, for instance, takes on a daunting set of commitments to guard some ecosystem. A sheepherder essentially commits to a role that puts the sheepherder as role-player in a service-provider position vis-à-vis a stable group of domesticated animals. Religious leaders generally assume a stewardship role. Academics often find themselves guarding some well-bounded knowledge asset.

- Agency—The roles based on the institution of agency provide for the role-player to act on behalf of an organization, or another role-player.

- Appointment—Appointment into a service-role is typical of the heads of governmental agencies, ambassadors, and the like. But appointment is also a fairly common manner of becoming a role-player, where some authorized role-player reaches out and taps someone into service.

- Self-selection—There are times when it's possible to appoint or select oneself into a service-role, without the permission or agreement of others. A citizen who steps in to pull a motorist from a burning wreck has self-selected into that service-role. It might seem that volunteering is self-selection, and some-times it is. At other times, however, there are qualifications that must be met, even to volunteer.

Service Types

Services form the basis of service-roles, and here we list a set of generic types of services. This list explores many types of services performed by role-players, but it is far from exhaustive. These types take on different characteristics according to the industry or domain of the organization, as well as APQC-like areas of functionality:

- Leading—Starting from its foundational days, every organi-zation depends significantly on the service-roles of leadership. Leading an organization is a very complicated type of service that usually includes many specific services provided by potentially many role-players.

- Envisioning—Part of leadership is generally recognized as the ability to envision the future of the organization, and to paint the picture of where it is headed. However, the ability to form compelling visions of the future is not limited to the founder or leader, and an organization can benefit from allowing visionary thinkers to emerge at various levels.
- Pathfinding—Beyond the envisioning and general leadership services, the pathfinding service depends on the ability to surmount obstacles, and anticipate snags and workarounds.
- Managing—A distinction is often drawn between leadership and management. For purposes of this list we'll just say that management is largely about the resource bargain that creates the ability for various parts of the organization to function adequately.
- Controlling—Much of what we see of organizational behavior is about encouraging and stimulating participation; let's not forget the opposite service provided by role-players whose job is to control particular aspects of the organization or environment. A part of marketing is to control the use of the branding icons, colors, and so on. A part of the CIO service-role is to control IT maintenance spending. The Controller's role is … well, you get the picture!
- Gatekeeping—A special type of control service is gatekeeping, whether performed by the night watchman at the warehouse, or the executive assistant for an executive. Gatekeeping services are fundamental in an age where cyber security is an increasingly important issue.
- Teaching—This is fairly straightforward, except that teaching as a service-role structure can take on many forms within organizations. There is obviously the dedicated training role, from inside or outside the organization. But there are unlimited opportunities for people to take on mentoring and informal teaching roles, where these service-roles may switch on any given day, based on the subject of learning. One of the forms of teaching to keep in mind is the large set of services involved in marketing, which is essentially an educational

service, teaching potential constituents about the advantages of the services offered by the organization.

- Diagnosing—A whole section of this book is dedicated to diagnosing the health of organizations, so here we'll just mention that the organization can benefit greatly from many sets of eyes and ears on the alert for conditions that depart from healthy parameters.

- Influencing—From a sales perspective, we often hear about the different kinds of buyers, for example, initiators, users, influencers, buyers, deciders, and gatekeepers. So we recognize the influencing role in sales. But there are many other ways that role-players as influencers can be encouraged, solicited, or merely tolerated in an organization.

- Selling—Speaking of various forms of buyers (and various forms of influence), consider the whole range of roles and role-nets involved in the services of selling, from prospecting, to lead generation, to "coaching the sale," to closing the sale.

- Persuading—Consideration of the selling service leads naturally into an even more pervasive service-role—that of persuasion. One of the hallmarks of the successful organization is the ability to persuade people to participate in all the ways we are outlining here. So the ability to persuade is really fundamental to your healthy organization.

- Documenting—The fidelity of organizations depend greatly on the service of documentation, in all forms of media from writing to video. Documenting is a very important service, included in many roles throughout the organization.

- Encouraging—A service that is often overlooked consists of simply encouraging others in their respective labors. This can take the form of ceremonial encouragement, or quiet recognition of efforts above and beyond the expectation or duty.

- Creating—The service of creation takes many forms. We tend to think of this as the inventive and innovative activities of the R&D department, but many service-role structures provide the opportunity to express creativity. A healthy organization tends to be one where people throughout its ranks have the opportunity to enhance their participation with satisfying creativity.

- Relating—The ability to make connections of all kinds is a service that is incorporated into many service-role structures throughout the organization. We can think of this as the ability to recognize patterns, and do appropriate matching of situations with patterns of response.

- Relaying—Sometimes the only service that is needed at the moment is a direct pass-through of a message or object. From a technology perspective, this looks like a hub or router, or even a software enterprise service bus. But there are also people throughout the organization who perform as reliable relay points of information to others. This, of course, was a much more pervasive service-role of "middle management" in the days before widespread electronic communications.

- Fueling—We have suggested that fuel of an organization is enthusiastic participation. So a key service, which the healthiest organizations know how to foster, is the ability to inspire other role-players to increased levels of enthusiasm.

Focal Point

Service-role structures almost always form around things of value to the organization. These are focal points that provide the context for services offered and performed by the players in various service-role structures. This could be an infinitely long list, because the "thing" that provides context for a service-role can be arbitrarily large or small, and arbitrarily complicated. A few examples are provided here to get the idea across, and leave further expansion to your imagination:

- Real estate—Land has been a primary concern of most organizations throughout the history of organizations. Places to work, places to extract raw materials (mines, wells, etc.), places to grow crops, places to store goods, and so on. Service-roles have evolved to improve, protect, and acquire the organizational property in terms of land and improvements to the land.

- Business interest—Service-roles proliferate with respect to stakeholder interests in business value, and the increase of business value.
- Capital—Capital can be a resource beyond effort applied to create valued services. Increasingly various forms of capital are being recognized, such as, social capital, intellectual capital, natural capital, and so on. For instance, the focal point of intellectual capital provides the context for role-player involvement in the area of ideas, and the expression and documentation of ideas.

Results

In addition to the service-types and focal points we've listed we very much need to consider the results produced by a provider of a service-role as part of co-creation of value. A service-role generally exists for the purpose of producing a type of result for a type of recipient. Expected results are at the very heart of service-role definition, and bring almost infinite variety to bear. This varies by market niche, the business function under consideration, as well as the focal point for the service; so for our purposes, we'll just mention a few results, along with their corresponding focal points:

- Within the context of intellectual capital, for instance, results can include patents, publications, courseware, case studies, methods, reference architectures, worked examples, and so on.
- Within a more tangible focal area, such as manufacturing, the result expected from a role-player might be maintenance of a robot, delivery of subassemblies to the assembly line, receiving parts from suppliers, and so on.

Image Postures

The idea of an image posture stems from how role-players see themselves, or desire others to see them. Again, we are far from exhaustive in our listing here, but rather suggestive of the underlying image aspects that go into service-role definition, and matching of role-players to the service-roles they play:

- Champion—Many people enjoy the self-image of champion of some idea or initiative. This is not limited to formal leaders and managers who stand up for the organization. It can be a very healthy situation where role-players are encouraged to act as advocates on behalf of business improvements, specific clients, and so on.
- Hero—The hero image differs from the champion by focusing on the personal strength and endurance of the role-player, rather than a particular cause or initiative. Heroic management wants to be seen as constantly fighting dangers, and prevailing by sheer force of will. This image posture, if unchecked, can be a contributor to unhealthy conditions.
- Martyr—A more extreme form of hero image can be observed as the martyr. Those taken with this image of themselves feel beset from every side by forces aiming to do them harm. The martyr image can become very damaging to the overall health of an organization, accompanied as it often is by self-fulfilling prophesies of disaster lurking around every corner.
- Follower—The follower image is actually very common, but not widely celebrated. However, there are factors that make good followers, and good followers are key to the health and success of organizations (Len Fehskens, personal communication of a presentation entitled "Why Do People Follow Leaders?" 2015).
- Good soldier—The good soldier is the image of a follower who is particularly loyal and devoted to the cause. This can focus a number of motivations in many people.
- Sidekick—The sidekick is close to the seat of power, and always ready to take up the cause of the hero or the champion.

- Comedian—The court jester is a well-known figure in history and literature, and for good reason. There is often real truth in humor, and the ability to break the tension of stressful situations through humor can be a powerful factor in the health of any organization.

Motivations

A role-player may become involved with certain service-role structures because of any number of possible motivations. A fairly extensive, but by no means exhaustive, set of motivations are listed below. Bear in mind that the same role-player may be motivated in more than one of these ways.

- Monetary—The monetary motivation causes a role-player to take on a service-role for monetary gain. This may not be the only motivation, but sometimes money acts as a stand-in for a set of underlying motivations.
- Creative—There are people who are completely, or somewhat, motivated by the ability to perform creative activities. There are service-roles in organizations that carry expectations of creativity in the services to be performed. Those who are motivated by creativity will be drawn to, and satisfied by, service-roles that offer the creative outlet they crave.
- Control—Some people just like to be in control. This is a psychological factor that is very strong in some people who are typically very risk averse. There are service-roles built around control-oriented services. Control-oriented people provide the best fit for control-oriented roles (or do they?). This can be a very healthy fit in certain organizational niches, not so healthy in other situations.
- Entrepreneurial—The entrepreneurial motivation has outlets in pure startups, as well as new service development (including skunk-works) within established organizations. An interesting phenomenon can be observed over and over.

One might call this serial entrepreneurialism. This motivation can be tremendously valuable, but may need to be managed carefully to maintain a healthy balance.

- Altruistic—Altruistic motivation can be a true phenomenon. This does not mean an altruistic person does not seek meaningful rewards for what they do. It's just that for some people the satisfaction of helping others is exactly the reward they seek. Does your business have a place for services that are offered by those who are motivated by altruism? This is definitely food for thought.

- Conformance—For a smoothly running, healthy business, there is a place for some people who are actually motivated to conform to various norms. People may be motivated to conform to a norm, even if the norm is to be "avant-garde."

- Ideological—An ideological role-player demonstrates commitment to some ideas and causes, even to the point of challenging entrenched power structures.

- Traditional—A role-player motivated by tradition believes that the role in question is simply the right thing to do, just because it's always been done that way.

- Personal attraction—Personal admiration, attraction, or friendship can be the basis for assuming voluntary or business service-roles. One way to talk about this basis for role and role-net formation might be to call it charisma based.

- Intellectual—Service-role definitions based on intellectual disciplines or field of study can create a common basis for role-players to align with academic institutions, as teachers and learners. These disciplines then carry over to the workplace, as practitioners of various types find themselves involved with roles that include corporate commitments and professional commitments. An example is the researcher who wants enough money to live, but really wants to work on cool things, keep nonstandard office hours, and a personal dress code.

- Loyalty—Those motivated by loyalty may take on a service-role in repayment of previous favors, some traditional relationship, or personal attraction.

- Superficial—A superficial motivation may attract a role-player, but with the result of weak to nonexistent perseverance on the part of that person.
- Fear—Do you want people in your organization who are motivated by fear? Have you considered what they fear, and why you believe this to be desirable?
- Coerced—People are forced to play the service-role of taxpayer, prison inmates are forced to play certain compliant roles, and military conscripts are forced to march into battle.
- Antagonism—Sometimes the only motivation for a role-player is some kind of antagonistic attitude toward a situation, another role-player, the competition, and so on. In such cases the service to be rendered may be more of an antiservice, such as revenge.

Implications for the Role-Player

A key to understanding the structure and dynamics of organizations is the fact that agreeing to become a role-player carries real implications for the person entering into such an agreement. Any role-player may have to deal with:

- Expectations—Once a person becomes a role-player, there may be any number of expectations triggered in the minds of other people. These have to do with the services to be performed within that role, and essentially all the aspects of the service-role definition.
- Responsibility—Not only are there expectations of performance, but, based on the governance mode, the level of responsibility may be required and may even lead to sanctions for nonperformance, and so on.
- Commitment—Taking on a service-role implies that the role-player is committed to everything stipulated by the service-role definition.
- Constraint—Not only might there be expectations, commitments and requirements, but service-role definitions often place constraints on role-players' behavior—no drinking on the job, no dating coworkers, and so on.

Levels of Involvement

Service-roles carry explicit and implied levels of involvement. It is important to design service-roles where motivations and levels of involvement line up appropriately. A service-role with a high level of involvement but low motivating power is liable to be performed half-heartedly, and with high turnover rates. Here are some levels of involvement to consider:

- Extent—Some service-roles are more wide ranging and diverse than others in terms of commitments, services, and expectations.
- Strength—Independent of the diversity, some service-roles exert varying degrees of power over the role-player to perform services and keep commitments
- Time demand—Time demand of service-roles can be analyzed, both in terms of the service-role definitions themselves, and in terms of time actually demanded of the role-player.
- Emotional intensity—In addition to time demands, service-roles exert differing demands on the emotions of role-players. In competitive situations, or when the consequences are high, or when human well-being is at stake, the emotional aspects of the service-role demands can be very intense.
- Density—Density refers to the overall level of participation in roles, with their collective demands on the role-player.

Governance Modes

Role structures conform to various governance modes, which tend to be dictated by the overall mission and posture of the organization as a whole.

- Prestructured—A formal job description illustrates the typical prestructured role. Similarly, learner service-roles in many educational institutions have a lot of specified structure.

- Negotiated—Some service-role definition situations allow negotiation in the opening stages of a relationship. Examples include contractor and consulting relationships with business entities. Some service-role definitions remain in a negotiated state for their duration. For instance, negotiating and renegotiating service-roles lies at the heart of Steve Haeckel's adaptive enterprise prescription (Haeckel 1999).

- Situational—In times of great stress service-role structures emerge seemingly out of nowhere. Yet, there seem to be patterns of these situational structures, such as the well-known neighbor helping neighbor pattern. Sometimes service-role structures appear in an opportunistic manner, as when a newsworthy event provides motivation for souvenir markets. Sometimes there are service-roles that form around the bricolage situation, where roles and role-nets form in order to make use of whatever is readily at hand. Fluid service-role structures form and morph constantly in the realm of improvisation, exemplified by jazz musicians.

- Legally binding—Certain roles, even if voluntarily assumed, impose legal restrictions or requirements upon the role-player.

- Permissive—A permissive service-role grants a significant degree of latitude in its performance.

- Imposed—One (very complex) service-role that is imposed on each of us, before we're even born is the service-role of citizenship. Royal families are born into even more complex and all-encompassing roles. Once in the military, personnel are subject to orders that impose service-roles upon them. Mandatory education rules impose student service-roles on young people up to a certain age. Service-role imposition can be in reverse as well. Based on any number of factors, certain people are excluded from serving in various roles.

- Empowered—An empowered service-role is granted decision making and resource allocation authority, with a promise that the organization will stand behind the role-player in the exercise of these powers.

Rewards

An important part of the service-role structure has to do with how performance of service-roles and roles will result in various kinds of rewards:

- Monetary—The monetary reward needs little explanation. The money-motivated role-player will be taking a close look at this!
- Advancement—A key reward in work-related roles, for most career-minded individuals has to do with the opportunity to advance themselves. Advancement can mean different things, but often means moving up in management ranks.
- Recognition—A few service-roles provide a real opportunity for recognition. The fame and fortune opportunity really appeals to a significant number of people, and especially given the current celebrity culture.
- Security—One of the service-role rewards may be promised or guaranteed longevity of the relationship. This kind of reward has become increasingly rare over recent years, looking back at an era when it was commonplace to expect "employment for life."
- Safety—A safety-oriented reward may not entail the most interesting of commitments, but at least it will not carry significant risks or dangers.
- Learning—A reward provided by certain service-role defini-tions can be seen as the opportunity to significantly increase experience-based knowledge, which in turn may lead to some form of upward mobility in the organization, or opportunities in other organizations.
- Mentoring—The mentoring reward can actually go in two directions. The mentee may gain benefits from support by a senior role-player, and the mentor may gain satisfaction of contributing to the future success of another person, and the organization itself.
- Protection—A particular service-role may provide cover for the role-player behind a well-placed sponsor or patron.

- Fun—Let's not forget that a major reason that people do things is for happiness, entertainment, and joy. In short, a reward offered by many service-roles can be the sheer fun of performing them.

Sanctions

The opposite of rewards are role-based sanctions for poor performance or malfeasance. Actual wrongdoing, including sabotage, embezzlement, and so on can result in any of the sanctions listed here, and even legal action, including incarceration.

- Withholding reward—Failure to perform a service-role according to expectations can result in withholding of some (part of a) reward.
- Confiscation—Sometime the sanction for bad performance in a service-role consists of confiscation of rewards already presented—colloquially, a clawback.
- Suspension—The right to perform the service-role is withdrawn, for some period of time by some authority.
- Reduction in pay—A more permanent impact on financial reward occurs with a reduced pay rate.
- Demotion—Reduction in rank may go along with monetary sanctions, and consequent loss of prestige, authority, and so on.
- Dismissal—A major sanction occurs when the role-player is removed not only from a role, but from an employment relationship altogether.
- Detainment—Most of the preceding sanctions have to do with work, but detainment, or confinement denotes legal sanctions that incarcerate the role-player in jail or prison, for violating some citizenship role.
- Fine—Fines generally charge money for a breach of expectations that do not rise to the level of demanding incarceration.
- Tacit—In addition to explicit, and officially recognized sanctions, many breaches of service-role expectations can lead to tacit, unofficial sanctions in the form of shunning, ridicule, bullying, and the like.

RACI-Type Roles

Any discussion of the subject of roles would be incomplete without consideration of the fairly standardized matrix of participation types for projects and processes. For the sake of completeness, here's a surprisingly long list of the participation types that are very commonly used in project management situations. These indicate various levels and types of involvement with the work, but perform a certain limited kind of service. These participation types intersect the service-role structure we have been examining here, and are focused on accountability and governance.

The most commonly mentioned scheme is RACI, which specifies those who are Responsible, Accountable, Consulted, and Informed about a project. A longer list of these accountability roles includes:

- *Accountable.* Delegates work and answers for completion
- *Agree.* Approves recommendations
- *Approver.* Makes decisions, and is responsible for failure
- *Assist.* Assists in completion of tasks
- *Authority.* Approves a decision
- *Consulted.* Those whose opinions are sought
- *Contributor.* Responsible for deliverables
- *Control.* Reviews the result of the activity
- *Decide.* Makes final decisions, commits group to action, ensures implementations
- *Driver.* Drives overall project like steering a car
- *Informed.* Impacted by the project and provided status and informed of decisions
- *Input.* Provides information and facts
- *Out of the loop (omitted).* Specifically not part of the task
- *Perform.* Carries out the activity, or defines who is accountable
- *Recommend.* Recommends answers to decisions
- *Responsible.* Has responsibility for the performance of the task
- *Signatory.* Approves decisions and authorizes hand-offs
- *Suggest.* Consulted for advice based upon expertise
- *Support.* Helps complete the task and supports implementation.

- *Task.* Identify who actually does the work
- *Verifier.* Checks against acceptance criteria

The list was extracted from a Wikipedia article that reviews a number of such schemes. This list is not grouped by scheme, but the Wikipedia article does provide such grouping, and provides references to the various sources (RACI 2015).

Service-Role Profile

Here is a simple form to use as a way of thinking about how the information about service-roles might be captured. A real tool for this purpose would need a more elaborate data model, based on the graphic above. There should be no assumption that such a form should be filled out exhaustively. This is just provided as a simple view into the characteristics list.

Service-role

Focal point	
Service type	
Service description	
Results	
Recipients	
Image posture	
Motivations	
Qualifications	
Tools	
Involvement scale	
Implications	
Institutional basis	
Governance modes	
Rewards	
Sanctions	
Providers	
RACI implications	

In the next chapter we will explore examples of these concepts and characteristics as they appear in higher-level structures of organization, from a job description to an entire business, and beyond.

CHAPTER 8

Applying Service-Role Structures

In this chapter we take a look at how the basic service-role, role-player, and role-net pattern gives rise to higher-level organizational forms. How does this pattern provide insight into job descriptions, departments, businesses, and other organization structures?

Job Descriptions

First of all, let's take a look at the service-role structures involved in a job, as recorded in a classic job description. In real-world organizations, the job description is the primary location for a view into service-role structures, and is mainly used in the hiring process. A job description automatically consists of a service-role, or a set of roles, and may also shed light on the composition of role-nets. The following publicly advertised job description, adapted and anonymized, illustrates these points.

Job Description—Enterprise Architect

(Our bank) is looking for an Enterprise Architect. As an enterprise architect you will embrace our digital banking vision and contribute leadership and broad and deep technical expertise to achieve that vision.

Responsibilities

- Partner with the business in the role of Enterprise Business Architect. Provide business insight and perspective, clarify

goals and strategies, guide implementation, analyze
business capabilities, and identify opportunities.

- Provide technical leadership on strategic enterprise
initiatives in the role of Enterprise Solution Architect.
Understand business objectives. Research potential
strategies. Architect and design solutions. Provide
leadership to guide implementation.
- Participate in business and technology strategic planning
processes. Guide business capability and technical
capability initiative roadmaps.
- Establish future-state enterprise-centric IT architectures
that consider business, information, application, infrastructure, and security perspectives.
- Focus on the consistency, completeness, interoperability,
and quality of solutions.
- Advocate for simple, standard, centralized, and automated
solutions to business needs.
- Mature the Enterprise Architecture practice.
- Stay current on technologies, technology trends and
directions, and best practices.

Requirements

- Proven track record of influencing change and leading
strategic enterprise IT initiatives to achieve well-defined
business objectives.
- Broad industry experience and broad IT leadership
experience.
- Deep hands-on technical expertise in multiple technical
domains.
- Demonstrated excellence in verbal and written communication. Can communicate effectively with business leaders
and technical experts at all organizational levels.

- Ability to listen for understanding, resolve conflicts, negotiate compromise, and collaboratively lead business leaders and project teams to optimal solutions.
- Ability to cultivate a shared strategic vision, articulate clear business objectives, and align the organization to achieve them.
- Experience in digital business transformation.
- Experience in enterprise application integration.
- Understanding of information architecture concepts that enable well-integrated transactional, analytical, and collaborative systems.
- Strong business and IT financial management acumen.
- Understanding of enterprise IT Service Management concepts.
- Ability to establish and lead IT Centers of Excellence.
- Banking or other Financial Services experience a plus.
- Bachelor's Degree in Engineering, Computer Science or related field.
- Eight+ years of experience in enterprise architecture and IT leadership.

Let's take a few minutes to examine this job description in light of our descriptions of the service-role structures and characteristics.

A long list of qualifications is provided in the *Requirements* section of the job descriptions. There are experience-based qualifications, including several that are actually labeled with the word "experience." In fact, a close reading reveals that almost all the qualifications, except for the requirement for the bachelor's degree certification, are most likely experience-based, including those that start "Ability to cultivate …," "Ability to listen …," and "Understanding of …." Presumably some of those could have been learned in a classroom or tutorial setting, but it seems unlikely that that's what the hiring authorities would be looking for in a candidate.

Notice that this description includes multiple explicit service-roles of "Enterprise Business Architect" and "Enterprise Solution Architect." There are indications of role-net expectations when the description talks about participating in planning processes, as well as partnering, advocating, and providing leadership. A number of specific services are mentioned, such as researching potential strategies, architecting and designing solutions, establishing future-state enterprise-centric IT architectures, maturing the Enterprise Architecture practice, and so on.

Some of the focal points can be inferred from the service names. At least it seems that this role-player is expected to create a couple of kinds of architectures (of solution, and of "future-state enterprise-centric IT"). It looks like one result would likely be a report on researching potential strategies, though it's possible the result might simply be an increase in knowledge on the part of the role-player. One very complicated result involves the EA practice itself, which this role-player will be responsible to mature.

So, who are the recipients of the services, whose needs or desires provide the implications of being the role-player under this job description? The job description does not go into much detail on the actual recipient role-players. Again, we can try to make inferences, such as that other role-players associated with the EA practice might be the recipients of the "maturing" activities of the holder of this job description. Nor does the description say anything about the reverse side of this issue, in terms of who owes services to the enterprise architect as the recipient. Maybe some players in the EA practice owe their best effort to become more mature in their practices?

We can assume that the institutional basis for this role is the simple employment relationship, since there is nothing specific about rewards or sanctions, stock options, bonuses, and so on. The governance mode is probably contractual, but the open-endedness of some of the service statements indicates there may be a fair amount of empowerment. In terms of levels of involvement we might assume a professional level of time demand, without emergency stress levels for the job as a whole.

What would you say the image posture of the ideal candidate would be? It looks like some combination of technocrat and executive, perhaps? Remember our lists of service-role characteristics are not all-encompassing, so feel free to imagine the ideal applicant or incumbent for this position. The same thing goes for motivations, although money is almost always a motive for job applicants, and some combination of intellectual, control, and creative motives might be reasonable to assume.

This kind of analysis can take time, but the results are well worth the investment. Everyone involved in such an exercise has a clearer idea of the fit between a person and a job description. In addition, job descriptions themselves can be made clearer to candidates, recruiters, and hiring managers alike. Of course some role profiles might not be overtly spelled out in public job descriptions—"We're looking for a traditionalist worker-bee." Not very enticing!

Departments

Another ubiquitous building block of the organization is the formal department. We might say that a department constitutes a permanent structure that provides a particular kind of service. At the departmental level it is possible to consider the service-roles of members of the department, and to consider the department itself as a collective role-player.

When we think about service-role structures of a department we need to focus on role-nets. On the one hand, the whole point of a department is specialization, so the set of services provided tends to be coherent and focused on particular focal points (monetary flow and accumulation for an accounting department, employee issues in an HR department). At the same time, as organizations get larger, departments themselves become large enough that they incorporate multiple job titles into their own internal network. By being specialized, they are only effective by participating at a departmental level with the other functional departments in the business or agency—in other words, providers and recipients at the department level are other departments. This means that departments need to manage internal and interdepartment role-nets.

Qualifications for individuals to be role-players in particular departments are typically related to formal learning and experience with the specialized services provided by the department. A big exception occurs in those organizations that rotate managers intentionally through multiple departments, so that they can experience various aspects of the organization on their way to the top.

Departments are fairly homogeneous in terms of image postures and motivations of the role-players. Levels of involvement are generally dictated by the types of service that the department provides to the organization as a whole. Think about the images, motivations, and involvement levels of the sales force, as opposed to, say, the IT department. From which departments do the CEOs of the world tend to emerge?

When there is a strong department structure, the institutional basis, governance modes, and implications for the role-player all tend to become more and more standardized over time, as service-roles coalesce into levels, with multiple players in very similar roles, providing very similar services. Issues of fairness about rewards and sanctions emerge, and perception of unfairness can loom as a serious health issue for your business.

As departments expand, they become entrenched in their internal and organizational power structures. As a result, when projects require formation of trans-departmental teams, the need increases for attention to the RACI-type roles, so that decision-making, communication, and implementation accommodate the various and diverse interests across the organization.

Whole Business

A business as a whole (a going concern) is where we focus on the issues we explored in earlier chapters, concerning viable systems and living organizations. We've said that living systems spontaneously emerge from patterns, maintain their identities in spite of part replacement, maintain boundaries within environments, and so on.

In that context, service providers and recipients at the business unit level are other living (viable) systems. Some of those are individuals, but many are peer-level organizations. Here it becomes important to recognize not only roles of your business, but also of the recipient and provider organizations as well. So, for instance, service-roles that do market research become important. This points toward a chapter on B2B services in the fourth section in this book.

There is really no point in enumerating service types and focal points at the business unit level, because this is subject only to human imagination and the ability to make a viable proposition to potential recipients. This is where industry and market positioning as well as niches and specialization become important. "We are attorneys focusing on the oil industry," for example.

The equivalent of an image posture at the viable system level is largely the subject of branding—that is, what image is the organization trying to project. Motivations at this level become very complicated, since all the role-players participating in the enterprise bring their own motivations. This leads to much time and effort spent trying to reach an agreement about vision and mission statements as well as efforts to balance money-making accountability with service obligations to various stakeholders who have wants and desires from the business.

Teams

When we look at the service-role structures of a team, typically we're talking about temporary or *ad hoc* role-nets. Of course we're not talking about sports teams, which *are* organizations, and in the case of professional sports, teams are also businesses in their own right. A team is typically a group formed to provide a specific service via a narrowly defined set of roles. Teams are generally intended to be temporary, and are likely to be cross-department and trans-disciplinary.

The provider-and-recipient relationships in a team may be relatively informal, and may even form during the formation of the team itself. The qualifications to play a role in a team may also be discovered or negotiated during the formation of the team, or even somewhat continuously.

The institutional basis for assigning people into team service-roles can often be by appointment, either by a designated team leader or by a manager or leader who chartered the team. Another characteristic of teams, however, is that the service-role assignment might actually be a matter of self-selection, either to join a team, or assume a service-role within the team. For instance a person may volunteer for the task of keeping notes of meetings.

From our incomplete list of types of services to be performed, it seems apparent that teams are not the best structures for managing anything on a continuous basis or controlling or gatekeeping. Most of the other service types on our list seem appropriate for teams as well as permanent organizational structures. The focal points of a team often include innovations or improvements, rather than more permanent responsibilities.

Image postures for team-based service-roles are generally of two types. Not surprisingly, the team structure is the ideal place for people to enhance their images as team players. This is especially true in organizations that put heavy reliance on teamwork and team building. The other image posture that aligns certain role-players within the team structure is that of leader. A team provides opportunities for players who aspire to permanent management or leadership roles to step up and demonstrate some leadership prowess. This very opportunity offers a strong motivation to establish teams, as testing and proving grounds for team players and leaders alike.

The motivations for assuming team service-roles tend to be quite different from seeking a more permanent job. Typically there are not direct monetary rewards for team participation, though this is a possibility. Motivations are more along the lines of self-development, visibility, novelty, and creativity, all which may add variety to predefined roles within job descriptions. Implications and associated levels of involvement include additional time demands and responsibilities. However, these may be more negotiable than permanent assignments.

Governance modes for team service-roles are often negotiated, or may be situational, permissive, and empowered. Rewards fall most often into the advancement, learning, and recognition types, or even fun, as in when the team is brought together to create a morale-boosting social event. Similarly, sanctions are not such a serious consideration for performance within team-based roles, but tend to be more tacit, such as loss of status among colleagues. Depending on the seriousness of the charter of the team, the RACI-type role accountabilities may be quite important. There is always a trade-off between the structured nature of a RACI approach versus the flexibility and temporary nature of many team efforts.

Additional Structures

You will never know all the informal roles in play within your business. In addition to job titles, departments, business units, and even recognized teams, it's easy to see that many of the service-role structures are not only informal but also *ad hoc* and created on the spur of the moment. They can also be covert, or even subversive to stated objectives and processes. What you don't want are whole underground structures of hidden role-players, eating away at morale and effectiveness. What you do want is to be able to benefit in a mutual way from the energy generated by the enthusiasm of people's natural affinity relationships.

Some of this seems obvious, in terms of affinity of interest. Birds of a feather flock together, as the old saying goes. Yet at the same time certain combinations of service-roles in role-nets introduce tension because of conflicting interests.

Playing the role of employee of a company and the role of a member of a labor union can exert conflicting forces on the role-player. Playing some role within an industry and at the same time within a regulator of that industry can also introduce conflicts of interest.

This entire topic of service-role structures presents major challenges to you as you perform the service-roles that you have taken on as a leader who is responsible to maintain the health of your business. This is what we focus on next.

CHAPTER 9

Service-Roles of Leadership

A key theme of this book is that viable organizations are built and emerge through the interaction of services rendered by people to each other. The network of service-roles that people perform as role-players forms the underlying structure. This applies throughout your business, and it applies equally to leaders and managers, including yourself. That is to say, leadership itself constitutes a complex set of service-roles, embedded in a complex role-net, whereby you perform unique services for your business and its participants. In this chapter we will discuss a few aspects of what is involved in being the role-player responsible to provide key leadership services, such as vision, strategy, decision-making, communication, leadership development, matching players to roles, CEO mindset, and minding the health of your business.

Vision-Setting

I'm thinking that there will be little disagreement with the idea that leadership services include articulating and communicating a vision for your business. If you're the entrepreneur of a start-up, this seems 100 percent intuitive.

From the heart of Silicon Valley there has emerged a strong Lean Startup movement, and its founder Eric Ries, confirms this concept of vision.

> Startups also have a true north, a destination in mind: creating a thriving and world-changing business. I call that a startup's vision. To achieve that vision, startups employ a strategy, which includes a business model, a product road map, a point of view about partners and competitors, and ideas about who the customer will be. The product is the end. Products change constantly through

the process of optimization, what I call tuning the engine. Less frequently, the strategy may have to change (called a pivot). However, the overarching vision rarely changes. (Ries 2011)

In an on-going concern, the vision still needs to be carried by the leader. This is almost the definition of what it means to truly be a leader. But there's a catch. While the vision may be "true north" as Ries suggests, even that may have to change within your business as time goes on, simply because the universe is changing around you. At a minimum, the vision will need to be communicated in a way that remains steady, as the whole universe changes around us. How to do this is anything but obvious. So the point is that hard work needs to be done, by the leader, to maintain focus on the vision. You need to put serious and sustained attention on this service to the business, which you really can't totally delegate.

Strategy (As Structure)

I like Steve Haeckel's idea that the leader is expected to articulate the reason for being (RfB), governing principles, and a high-level business design (Haeckel 1999). The RfB is very close to the "vision" we've just discussed, and experience confirms that it's a lot of work to get this right, so that it is understandable, compelling, and stands the test of time.

The high-level business design is a structure of key elements of the business, and their intended outcomes. To create such a structure, we ask "who owes what to whom?" in terms that consider the highest-level service-roles, in our parlance, and think backward from the results that they need to provide for customers and other recipients, including each other, in the context of the enduring vision. Such a structure will impact your organization chart, but is actually more fundamental in terms of what it takes to realize the RfB of your business.

The prescription includes the following five steps a business leader would take to produce an adaptive organizational system design.

1. Establish organizational purpose as an effect: a change to be created in an entity outside the boundaries of the organization being designed (NOT in terms of an internal objective).

2. Decompose (deconstruct) organizational purpose into subordinate subsystems of roles and outcomes. (*Do* NOT integrate existing roles, processes or capabilities into larger components).
3. Specify the interactions between roles as an exchange of outcomes and effects (NOT the actions of roles as a sequence of tasks and decisions).
4. Make roles interoperable and modular by using a standard protocol for negotiating, renegotiating and tracking commitments to outcomes (NOT by relying on the transmission of orders down the chains of command).
5. Measure enterprise success in terms of organizational purpose (NOT in terms of the rewards for success) (Haeckel 2010).

One way to think about your challenge as a leader, is that you want to tilt the balance of design versus emergence (Chapter 3) in favor of conscious design, while harnessing the emergence that occurs as your business takes on a life and mind of its own. This a matter of balance, because, while you don't want the business to drift in unproductive directions, you also really don't want to be perfectly successful in imposing a design only to find out you were wrong, because of a blind spot or for whatever reason, and to feel that if you'd listened to the perceptions from the perimeter, the business could have been more successful.

Decision-Making

You, as the leader, also must perform the service-role of key decision-maker, correct? Well, maybe, but this does not mean that you should assume the service-role of the *only* decision-maker. In fact, we might say that one of the leader's most important service-roles includes the correct level of delegation and empowerment of distributed decision-making.

From the discussion on the decision making process, we can derive the need for these two Decision Making Roles:

1. Decision makers, who make the decisions, and
2. Advisors are 'decision coaches' who guide and facilitate the decision making process.

Decision makers carry the responsibility to familiarize themselves with the business context and decision model, and work with the decision process to arrive at the best decisions for the business. In many cases, decision makers work closely with modelers to frame and flesh out the model, and downstream to drive the implementation and results. (Saxena 2012)

Communicating—It's Bidirectional

One way to look at this leadership issue is that your primary service to the business is maintaining a balance between subsidiarity and coherence. I know that's a mouthful, but the principle of subsidiarity means pushing as much real-time control and decision-making out to the edge of your business, where it touches the marketplace. The balance with coherence means that you want to delegate as far down as possible while still maintaining an understandable message and consistent customer interaction. This viewpoint recognizes that "Nobody is smarter than everybody" (Collins 2013), so you want to involve the people whose eyes and ears are sensing the daily interaction, the co-creation, the structural coupling, of the business and the market. At the same time, leaders are in a unique position of oversight and responsibility for coherence of identity and direction. Achieving this balance is at the heart of the services you perform as a leader.

The Ladder of Responsibility

One of the most important points of balance for business leaders concerns the mindset that you bring to the leadership role. However, it is the norm in smaller businesses and startups for the founder and owner to be a passionate performer, who starts a business to pursue that passion, without necessarily going through a series of training and promotion experiences to build the mindset and expertise of a seasoned CEO.

A good starting point for this discussion is found in the book *The Leadership Pipeline* (Charan, Drotter, and Noel 2011). This book generally uses management and leadership interchangeably, whereas others are careful to make a clear distinction. Be that as it may, the key point of the book is that the skills and mindset of different levels of responsibility have distinctly different characteristics, that each can be learned, and that they build on each other. The book refers to this structure as an "architecture" for the human side of the business, and also a "pipeline," as the title states. The following rough and incomplete summary of this architecture provides an idea of the kinds of transitions that need to occur along the trajectory to ever-higher levels of responsibility:

Manage self—Young people entering the workforce first need to learn to function well at work by making new, productive habits for themselves. If they're successful, and have the qualifications, they can become superstar performers and obvious candidates for promotion. Or so it seems.

Manage others—Once people are promoted to the position of managing other role-players, they need to step out of the superstar spotlight and assume the service-role of getting things done via other people. This can be hard for superstar performers, who are often tempted to fall back into the comfort zone of superstars. As they emerge as successful leaders of performers, the next promotion looms.

Manage managers—Up a level from managing others, is the role of manager of managers, or leader of leaders. Here the challenge becomes how to turn the next generation of superstars into managers of people. This requires performance of service-roles that balance mentorship of new managers with keeping a pulse on the front line. Success here leads to … well, you know the drill!

Manage a function—Sometimes the organization is large and complicated enough to reach a pinnacle of managing a specialty, such as HR or IT (think CIO). The priorities change again to groom the managers of managers, while interacting and negotiating with their peer functional leaders. This may be where lateral moves occur for those who are being groomed for higher office, as it were.

Manage a business unit—At the business unit level, a leader's service-roles have a still wider scope requiring the ability to balance all functions, not just one's own specialty. Sometimes this is the top, but in the largest organizations, as the authors point out, there may be a "group" level as well.

Manage a corporation—Ultimately, a few leaders reach the top (if that's the way you look at it) as the CEO, the leader, the visionary, the strategist. Those service-roles (visionary, strategist, etc.) require shifts of perspective as much as the previous steps up the ladder. The smaller the organization, the fewer the possible steps, and the less preparation along the way. And, oh by the way, this is exactly where the entrepreneur, or new business owner might actually *start*! With no particular preparation in managing managers, managing a function, or managing a smaller business unit within a larger institution. Gulp!

Balancing CEO and Expert Mindsets

As just noted, at the top of the organization is the leader, no matter what the size and age of the organization. That leadership service-role is largely responsible for providing the service of crafting and communicating vision and strategy. Even the one-person shop cannot escape all the services that go along with running a business. These leadership services will not be performed properly if the mindset of leadership is stuck at one of the earlier levels of maturity, such as being the go-to, superstar performer in the field. At the same time, that passion for the work should really not be denied. Almost certainly you are where you are because of the love of the work, the desire to satisfy customers and clients, the satisfaction you get from knowing that you are the best at what you do, which may be what motivated you to get into business in the first place.

What do you think of when you think of a CEO? The celebrity CEO? Do certain famous names come to mind? Jack Welch? Meg Whitman? Richard Branson? Lou Gestner, Sam Palmisano, or Ginny Rometty? Steve Jobs? Henry Ford? Warren Buffet? I'm not going to try to explore what these people may have in common. I'll just let those images sink in, and ask you to think which, if any of them seem to be perfect role models for the leader of a business?

No matter how different CEOs may be in personality, education, and experience, I think we can agree that the great ones stay in our minds as the faces of their companies. They carry the image, the brand, and the story of their organizations. They set the tone for the culture, and what it means to be a member of their teams. For any business to experience a healthy future, and rise to its potential, there needs to be someone with the mindset of a leader to stand up and take the lead.

There are many ways to develop into that leader. It's not our purpose here to catalog all the aspects, and all the sources of help in that quest. But here are a few points to consider.

It is difficult under any circumstances to bear the responsibility for the vision setting and decision-making that provide guidance to your business. Yet, these are exactly the *services* you, as the leader, owe to the business, and to all of its participants. This becomes overwhelming if, at the same time, you are mired in the day-to-day firefighting and details. Setting and guiding the vision opens up the opportunities for the future growth and maturity of your business. Without the CEO mindset, it is all too easy for you to literally become the bottleneck. If you can't find the time to get away from the press of current events, then the business tends to stay at its current level or shrink and shrivel.

A big part of the problem is micromanaging everything that needs to be done. And why would you do that? You can answer that yourself, but if you're honest with yourself I'm sure that lack of trust is at the heart of the answer. Can you trust the people who are performing and managing, to do things the way you feel they should be done? Do they know how to interact with customers? Do they maintain your standards of quality? Can you trust all aspects of your business to operate smoothly when you take your eyes away? If not, this is a health issue of the highest priority.

The Hoppers Weigh In

Some important insight about the need for balance between managing and leading, and between the CEO mindset and the passionate expert mindset, is provided in a fascinating history of American business authored by two British authors, who just happen to be brothers.

> Leaders are characterized as charismatic figures who command loyalty and offer a vision – managers as dull, gray administrators. This is a false apposition—to be effective, a manager must be able to lead. It is possible to lead without fuss. (Hopper and Hopper 2009)

The best description of America's corporate chief executives in what the Hoppers call "the Golden Age" was provided by a quote in the book from Vassar professor, Mabel Newcomer, who states that the "big business executive" was:

> ... a native(-born) American, the son of a small, independent businessman. His family income was moderate. And such small jobs as he pursued during his boyhood were for extra spending rather than to help support his family. His parents managed to put him through college, with such contributions as he himself made to his own expenses through part-time employment. Upon graduation he obtained a fulltime job, with no assistance from his family. Thenceforth he was on his own. While still relatively young and inexperienced, he obtained a minor position with the corporation that he eventually headed, and he gradually worked up, through operations or production, to a vice-presidency, from which he was promoted to the presidency at the age of fifty-two.

The Hoppers observe that the Golden Age fostered the internal growth of leaders who truly, and at a gut level, understood and appreciated what the workers felt, how they were motivated, the esprit de corps within a band of brothers and sisters. They may have endured hardships, but that is what makes them unique, and gave them a sense of accomplishment. Can an outsider, educated in general theories of business management, ever have the visceral relationship to this kind of working organization? Can they gain this perspective, and the trust and rapport that go along with it?

The authors are relentless in their criticism of what they call "The Cult of the So-Called Expert," which is the doctrine that management itself is a specialty that can be taught, and that a well-taught manager should be able to manage in any context. Quoting again from the Hoppers, this passage beautifully summarizes the downside of the situation when business skews to the pure MBA model for leadership and management:

> Charles Protzman III, is a hands-on management consultant who attempts to re-teach Americans how to manage factory floors or their equivalent in other sectors of the economy. Having read a draft of this book, he has written to say how much he supports its

conclusions and recommendations, adding: 'In most companies that I have visited, and some where I have worked, there are shop floor workers who have been around for twenty or thirty years, supervised by "professional" managers, who have been there for eighteen months or less, some with MBAs and some without. When a new departmental head is appointed, he has no idea what the workers are doing—so the workers have to stop work to train him. They may try to explain to him the problems that they face but he is unlikely to do much about them because he does not want to upset his boss and endanger a future promotion. Then he will start implementing changes to respond to upper management's demands, in order to meet the month's or the quarter's financial projections'.

It is possible and common practice, to make a conceptual distinction between the role of leader and the role of a passionate performer. In reality, though, your success in balancing these two perspectives will have a significant impact on the health of your business. Can you do the things that are required of the CEO? Can you champion the vision? Can you lead your team into the future? Can you satisfy the need for ceremony? Can you perform the service-role of public spokesperson? And, at the same time, can you assure that your knowledge of the industry, the methods and techniques required for success, your passion for the work, are transmitted and followed by everyone who is doing the work that you love to do?

Matching Players to Service-Roles

Building on the need to balance CEO and expert mindsets, let's also consider the tricky issue of balancing key service-roles with the personal characteristics of key role-player assignments. This is conceptually straightforward—the health of your business will be stronger to the extent that people are allowed to play in service-roles where they feel a strong attraction. Without effective matching, you may end up with role-playing incoherence. It's important to be able to diagnose mismatches in order to get the help you need to maintain the health of your business.

The good news is that there are actually many systems and methods that claim to detect and record personality traits. There is substantial information available for many of these methods, including on-line tests on the Internet, and basic reporting of results for free, and of course, for a fee. The full methods for interpreting results, however, are not generally in the public domain, and many need certification for a practitioner to administer them. Here are just a few examples:

- The 34 Strengths profiling framework, apparently validated by the Gallup organization through interactions with over a million managers, focuses on areas where managers rate themselves strongest. Just to give a flavor of this technique few of the 34 strengths include: Adaptability—good at dealing with change, Empathy—good at dealing with the emotions of others, Futuristic—good at using foresight, Intellection—good at compressing complex concepts into simplified models, Learner—good at learning new things to feel successful, and one of my personal favorites WOO—good at persuasion, or "Winning Others Over").

- The main idea behind the Hartman Color Personality Assessment is that all people possess one of four driving "core motives." The driving core motives are classified into four colors that stand for power, intimacy, peace, and fun. Hartman believes the system is simple and at the same time profound in matching people whose core motives coincide with the requirements of service-roles.

- Myers Briggs® personality types theory (MBTI®) seeks to determine which of 16 profiles a person fits by combining where they fit on each of four scales of preferences, such as making decisions based on logic versus feelings. This framework is based on personality archetypes developed by pioneering psychiatrist Carl Jung. Myers Briggs is sometimes used in team-building, to get a balance of personality factors on a team.

- David Keirsey's Temperament Sorter model seems on cursory examination to be very similar to Myers Briggs. However

Keirsey, according to some sources, is measuring observable behavior, while Myers Briggs focuses on thoughts and feelings. This test attempts to sort people into four basic temperaments: the Artisan, the Guardian, the Rational, and the Idealist.

- William Moulton Marston, was a psychologist, lawyer, and inventor (who also invented a polygraph lie-detector, and created the Wonder Woman superhero). His DiSC system measures the behavioral traits of dominance, inducement, submission, and compliance. It is intended to show behavior in a particular environment, rather than simply personality assessment. Over the years a number of systems have been created and marketed, based on Marston's work.

There are many more personality, temperament, and behavior assessment systems, including the Belbin Team Roles and personality types theory, the FIRO-B® Personality Assessment model, Birkman Method®, and others ("personality" 2015).

The importance of getting a good match between individual people with the profiles of service-roles cannot be overstated. It would be wonderful if we could report that this is an exact and infallible science, but such does not seem to be the case. Which of these personality assessments might be the best for matching people with service-roles in your business? Much of the answer depends on your understanding of your situation, and how the methods seem to fit. There is also no substitute for a good relationship with a trusted practitioner.

Diagnostics, Anyone?

So here's the question: Do you spend anywhere nearly enough time performing the services of creating and communicating the vision, strategy, and plans for your business? Or are you constantly distracted from being able to perform the services of leadership? How much time do you spend overseeing, and even performing, the daily operations of the business? How many of these worries and pains are keeping you up at night: competition, costs, culture, customers, facilities, finance, laws and regulations, marketing and sales, personal feelings of burnout, planning for succession, procurement, products and services, quality, relationships, technology, workers and advisors? These are the burdens that we're talking about.

Where are you on the scale between a pure leadership position (CEO mindset) versus passion for the actual work of the business (expert mindset)? A lack of balance here may be hard for you to perceive, simply because you are so deeply involved. On the other hand, there may be some indicators that *only* you are able to perceive, possibly with some effective coaching, including how comfortable you feel interacting with the people on the edge of the business, or how comfortable you are with the ceremonial, public roles that are intrinsic parts of leadership. You may be harboring feelings that you're not getting everything out of the business that you hoped, that you're ready to sell out, that you're trapped, and can't take even a day of vacation. We obviously can't diagnose your particular situation here, but any of these indicators would be a great reason to spend a bit of time on achieving some real clarity.

The next section of this book deals with diagnosing the condition of your business. You will notice that a high percentage of this section consists of questions. This is not just to make your head hurt (though it probably will)! This is the nature of diagnosis, and much of the practical value of this book comes from development of a diagnostic mindset. You are the only one who really knows the answers to these questions, so at least in this section of the book we will avoid presuming to know the answers.

In this section, we will see how this diagnostic framework builds on various tried and true standard initiatives, as well as more current 21st century consulting methods and techniques.

PART III

Diagnosing Your Business

CHAPTER 10

Coaching Approach to Diagnostics

Let's begin the discussion of diagnosing your business by looking at the techniques and value of a coaching approach to diagnosing the health of business. There are not too many hard and fast recommendations in this book, but this is one. The coaching approach is probably the most powerful and effective overall diagnostic technique. This is because coaches are trained (at least the ones who have had training!) to understand that no one can truly know what any other person has experienced in life or exactly how another person's mind works. So the coaching approach to achieve clarity in the midst of daily dilemmas and ambiguities is to bring out answers in the unique context of the individual person's mind and experience.

The coaching perspective is distinct from therapy, which looks backward in time to try to find the origins of problems in the past experiences of a client. Coaching assumes that clients are healthy, mature individuals, who can benefit from the perspective of an outside view that helps overcome blind spots and provides clarity about the range of opportunities and approaches that might be available.

Core Competencies of Coaching

In order to summarize the service offered by a trained coach, let's use a framework of the 11 core competencies, as taught by the International Coach Federation (ICF) ("Core Competencies" 2015). Competence in these skills and perspectives is valuable, whether the coaching relationship is focused on business or career purposes, life coaching, relationship coaching, grief coaching, or any of the various other coaching specialties.

Our focus is on coaching for the purposes of diagnosing the health of your business, which is how we present the core competencies.

Meeting Ethical Guidelines and Professional Standards

The ICF stresses ethical standards very heavily. Coaches who have gone through a rigorous training and certification program are all acutely aware that the marketplace has exhibited a high degree of tolerance for people who loosely apply the word "coach" to their work. Partly, this stems from the fact that the term was borrowed originally from the world of sports and then applied very widely to the kinds of situations noted above. ICF, as a professional organization, put ethical standards at the heart of the coaching profession.

Key to the ethical guidelines is the distinctions among coaching, consulting, psychotherapy, and so on. A coach needs to be on the alert to refer clients to other support professionals as needed. This aspect of coaching lends itself perfectly to the diagnostic work of business health. There is a large, but disjoint, marketplace of service providers who address many aspects of business health. A coach who is skilled at establishing clarity about business issues does well to be equally knowledgeable about the range of services that bring specific expertise to specific business issues.

Establishing the Coaching Agreement

Establishment of clear expectations and agreements applies in the beginning of a coaching relationship and in every interaction thereafter. It's hard to over stress the deep services perspective implied by this behavior. With a competent coach, your progress toward business health will be maintained uppermost in the relationship.

Establishing Trust and Intimacy with the Client

The coaching relationship focuses on genuine concern for your welfare and future. This encompasses the health and welfare of both you and your business and must be based on a trusting relationship. This forms the basis for deep understanding of business issues and makes it possible for meaningful prescriptions of health-promoting business services, as well as the creation of new habits of thought and action.

Coaching Presence

A coach should present the image of a mature and empathetic individual. The coach should come across as very knowledgeable, but also flexible enough to follow an inquiring line of thought wherever it might go, without preconceptions.

Active Listening

A diagnostic service tailored to your situation stems from an ability to listen carefully and, as a result, to understand clearly the implications of discussions and observations. ICF talks about summarizing, paraphrasing, and reiterating the client's words for purposes of clarity and understanding. However, it's not enough to simply parrot words back like a kind of human Eliza program. The key is to test continually for clear understanding, in an effort to untangle the complications of running a business.

Powerful Questioning

The real key to a coaching-style relationship is the ability on the part of the coach to ask questions that evoke discovery, insight, commitment, and action, and that truly challenge the client's assumptions. Powerful questioning involves open-ended questions that encourage exploration of the bigger picture and underlying issues. The answers might actually surprise both you and the diagnostician coach.

Direct Communication

In addition to the focus on powerful questions (20 percent of the time) and active listening (80 percent of the time), the ability to communicate clearly and directly is essential. Direct communication is required to reframe issues and situations in a way that captures your attention. Direct communication may involve creative use of metaphor and analogy but always in the service of absolute clarity.

Creating Awareness

The ability to integrate and evaluate multiple sources of information is where the diagnostic coach provides the basis for awareness. Various analytical and communication methods, coupled with wide-ranging and deep knowledge of the health-providing services in the marketplace, come together to help you gain awareness of the needs of your business and make an effective match with what's available.

Designing Actions

Actions to improve business health all revolve around establishing new habits of thought and action, and reaching out to expert service-providers to achieve healthy balance points. The expert coaching diagnostician works with you to explore alternative ideas and solutions, to evaluate options, and to make appropriate decisions. Effective commitment to action relies on active experimentation and self-discovery, not simply a recitation of the coach's favorite remedies!

Planning and Goal Setting

Even though any action plan must be *your* plan, you can benefit from the help of a coaching diagnostician in developing and maintaining a business health plan. Such a plan should drive toward results that are specific, measurable, attainable, really needed, with true time commitments (which you might recognize as a variation on the proverbial SMART goal framework). If the coaching and consulting relationship extends beyond a one-time diagnostic event, you might expect the diagnostic coach to be involved with plan adjustments as warranted by circumstances. Note that professional coaches are actually trained to recognize that part of their service is to help "the client identify and access different resources for learning (e.g., books, other professionals)."

Managing Progress and Accountability

This particular competency applies to a relationship that extends over time, where the coach acts as a kind of general practitioner for business health. In an extended relationship, the coaching diagnostician can be expected to maintain attention on what was agreed in the action designs and plan while leaving responsibility with you to take the appropriate actions.

Habits of Thought and Action

One of the most basic requirements of running a healthy business is the ability to form effective habits of thought and habits of action. You need to develop habits that are consistent and balanced so that you're not thinking and saying one thing but actually acting in ways that conflict with what you espouse. This is trickier than it sounds and essentially requires a special kind of homeostasis. In other words, we need to amplify the factors and messages that build consistent and balanced habits of thought and action and attenuate those that work at cross-purposes to achieving desired results.

One of the key messages of this book is to form a habit of thinking about every aspect of your business from the viewpoint of service. This change of thought habit will definitely be a challenge for almost everyone reading this. However, that habit of thought can clarify the relationship between the business and its leadership while tapping into the potential of all participants.

Making and Breaking Habits

The key to the coaching experience is the ability to form new habits of thought and action. One approach is the "Not-To-Do" list, which catalogs the things we need to *stop* doing (in other words, habits to break). But, while this is a cute idea, there's a good reason not to overly focus on the not-to-do's, based on current understanding of how the brain works.

Everyone knows that trying to break a bad habit is devilishly hard. Of that there is no doubt. The stop-smoking industry, the diet industry, the self-help industry are all built on the fact that it is indeed very difficult to break habits that have taken hold in our minds. As a result, there is a lot of repeat business in those industries!

Science is still in the early days of fully understanding the workings of the human mind. However, recent advances in the science of the brain are starting to give us new knowledge of how habits are created and how they can replace destructive behaviors. Based on recent brain research, we have better ideas of why this is so hard and, more importantly, what we can do about it.

One way of thinking about this is the so-called habit loop, which emphasizes how rewards reinforce habitual behavior and prescribes ways to achieve the same reward with different behavior. A lot of this has to do with how the reward is defined. If the reward is itself the enjoyment of a cigarette, then changing behavior to get that particular reward is not the answer. However, recognition of different rewards may be the answer. In one case study, a manager established the reward of experiencing an intensive international business trip. The behavior required to achieve *that* reward served to overwhelm a number of more trivial habits that appeared to get in the way (Duhigg 2012).

Another perspective is that reinforcing mechanisms in the brain make it difficult to *break* a habit. "The more we focus on a problem we have, the more ingrained we make it." This suggests that business leaders (acting as coaches) can benefit by helping people focus on the process of *thinking itself*. If employees (or clients) can think about their own thought processes, they can create new habits of thought and action. Specific advice on how to help a client or employee form new habits can be summarized by the acronym, CREATE—understand their Current Reality, Explore Alternatives, and Tap into their own Energy for positive change (Rock 2006).

Another approach, with wide applicability, is the happiness habit. Shawn Achor spent over a decade at Harvard University, first as a student and then as proctor and instructor. During that time he wondered why so many Harvard students had so much stress-related unhappiness when they had so much going for them. His basic finding was that success is based on happiness and not the other way around and that happiness is very much a mindset that can be learned (Achor 2010).

A very important insight is that brain science has overturned the previous belief that human minds are formed early in life and then it is nearly impossible to change them. Now the prevailing scientific notion is neuroplasticity, based on countless demonstrations of the flexibility and teachability of mental faculties throughout life. Many studies have shown that happiness in the workplace leads to measurable improvements in productivity and innovation. Workplace happiness can be increased by stressing things to look forward to, consciously creating opportunities to perform acts of kindness, infusing positivity into the surroundings, exercise, spending money on others, and consciously exercising key strengths.

People tend to become fixated in one way of seeing the world, positive or negative. If work continuously involves a negative or critical stance (such as a tax agent spending all working hours looking for tax errors and evasions), minds will be so trained to look for errors that this expectation carries over into other aspects of life. The good news is that the brain can be retrained to become more aware of positive happenings and opportunities, thereby creating health-promoting habits of happiness. Simple exercises like writing down three positive events every day can create a habit of positive thinking.

It is important to turn habits of thought into habits of action. William James, the famous psychologist, claimed that human beings are "mere bundles of habits." The problem is that will power alone provides a limited energy source to enforcing positive actions. The "path of least resistance" is a powerful magnet, which can lead to endless procrastination. On the other hand, it is possible to design situations so that desired activities require less resistance to activate (such as the advice "Sleep in your gym clothes" to remove a barrier to start exercise each morning).

Achor proposes social investment in the workplace, since the worst thing to do when times get tough is to hunker down in the rugged individual mode. In hard times, we need the support of our social networks most of all. Positive and negative attitudes, as manifested in public actions, are both very contagious. Achor quotes Daniel Goleman as saying, "Like secondhand smoke, the leakage of emotions can make a bystander an innocent casualty of someone else's toxic state." Those we influence through positive attitudes and interactions, in turn, influence others in a similar way. This mechanism traces back to the "mirror neurons" that light up in our brains as we observe the experience of others just as if we are experiencing the situation ourselves. Achor concludes, "By making changes within ourselves, we can actually bring the benefits of the Happiness Advantage to our teams, our organizations, and everyone around us" (Achor 2010).

A Structure of Inquiry

How about a simple way to help you think more like a coach? Figures 10.1 and 10.2 may help you perform some coach-like self-diagnosis of your relationship with your business.

Start by thinking about the motivations that got you going down the leadership path where you find yourself today. What was the desired situation that you envisioned? What did that make you feel like, to imagine yourself in the successful position that you desired? How can you imagine the processes that were effective in getting you to that position?

Now think about your current reality. How close is it to what you imagined and desired? Take a close hard look at the gap between the two. What feelings are caused by your experience of the gap? What is the state of the processes in your business and in your life? What outcome are those processes actually producing? Who are the key players in your life and business, and what roles are they actually playing? And what kind of time are you personally spending dealing with the current situation.

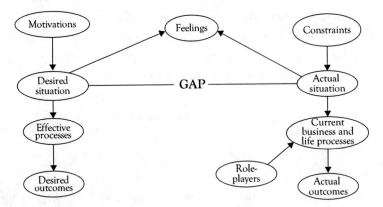

Figure 10.1 Desires and reality

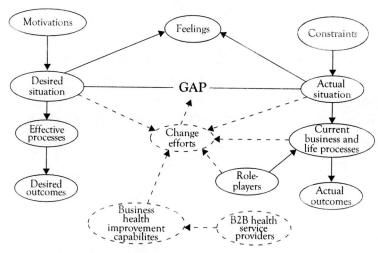

Figure 10.2 Addressing the gap

Now, it's probably true that you can really only go so far in trying to coach yourself. Eventually you will run up against blind spots or what you don't know that you don't know. Consequently, it is important to look for that good coaching diagnostician, who is an expert in the competencies we've just outlined here.

Ideally what you're looking for is a trained, professional coach, who also has the business knowledge and experience to help navigate through the complexity of the business services marketplace. One place to look is for a coach associated with one of several reputable business coaching franchises. However, it is important to keep in mind that the personal relationship is very important here, so it's always a good idea to take advantage of a "chemistry session," to see how you align on a personal and professional level. Be suspicious of anyone, even someone who takes a coaching perspective, who is unwilling to make referrals or prescriptions to service-providers outside of their own practice.

The heart of the matter is that you will really need to make some efforts to change. Most of the change, frankly, is likely to be in your own habits of thought and action. But you also need to involve those key role-players who are either helping you or holding you back. You will need to achieve new abilities, as your situation continues to evolve. And this is where the marketplace of B2B health services comes in. In the final section of this book we will cover the abilities that are needed to maintain balance in key areas as a leader and for your business.

But before we get there, let's take a look at a number of areas that may need to be diagnosed and several frameworks and methods for uncovering problem areas. As we go, we'll mention many of the kinds of services that are available, and we've already started that by talking about the value of certain coaching methods.

CHAPTER 11

Functional Areas Diagnostics

Having reviewed the value that a coaching approach can bring to the process of diagnosing business health, we now have a chance to see a bit of that approach in action. In the following sections a number of questions have been laid out, specifically to provide a chance to experience the power of the open-ended question.

The sections in this chapter are loosely based on a modified top-level structure of the APQC Process Classification Framework that we noted back in Chapter 1. It's not the only way to look at the functions of a business, but it provides a reasonable starting point, since we're not trying to be exhaustive in any event (APQC 2014).

Developing the Vision

As the leader of an enterprise we've seen that you perform some of the most important services that keeps the organization healthy. One service of leadership is developing a vision for the future. Earlier we described the fuel of the organization as the enthusiastic energy of its participants. Well, this is where enthusiastic energy starts. It is almost impossible for anyone other than a leader of the organization to have that kind of beneficial effect. On the other hand, low morale can often be attributed to the failure of leadership to provide a compelling and positive view of the future. So, some diagnostic questions:

- How do you develop your vision, and keep it fresh?
- How well do you articulate the opportunities to pursue?
- What strengths are you personally able to bring to bear?
- How fully do people in the organization buy into your vision?

Communicating the Vision

It's really not enough to simply develop a compelling vision. The vision needs to be communicated in a compelling way as well. It's probably not enough to write a vision statement that sounds like a committee effort, print copies, and tack them to every bulletin board in the office or shop. Tacking a vision statement on the bulletin board is itself not a bad idea, but how does the vision become a memorable reminder of the compelling story that people can really buy into?

- How do you communicate your vision throughout the organization?
- When you walk around, what are people talking about?
- Who are the most effective people to involve in communication of your vision?
- How would you rate the effectiveness of your vision communication process?

Strategy

Strategy goes beyond vision, to lay out an approach to achieving the vision. There was a time when strategy was regarded as a 5-year, or even 10-year plan. This is virtually impossible in these times of continually accelerating change. Yet it is part of the leadership service-role to provide guidance for the organization to move forward. So, with that in mind, let us consider the following diagnostic questions:

- How do you develop your strategy?
- How often do you revisit your strategy?
- As in the case of vision, how do you *communicate* your strategy throughout the organization?
- How would you rate the effectiveness of your strategy and communication processes?
- How well does your organization execute against the strategy?

Service Offering Development

Here we're talking about services that fulfill the RfB of your business. This also includes the products as a special case service where the coproduction of value occurs independent of time and distance, consistent with our general perspective of all-services-all-the-time.

- How do you develop new services?
- What is your method for articulating service offerings?
- How much of your innovation process is performed or supported by consultants?
- How's that working out?
- Which services are delivered in the form of 'products'?
- What is the main driver in the development of offerings?
- What interaction occurs between offering development and marketing?
- How would you rate the effectiveness of the offering development process?

Marketing

Marketing can be thought of as the education of your clientele on what you offer, so that they are attracted to do business with you. As with many other aspects of business, marketing practices are evolving very quickly. Our purpose here is not to provide a tutorial on 21st Century marketing, but the subjects of social media, digital marketing, growth hacking, and content marketing are worth looking into, as indicators of the direction that marketing is moving.

- What is your approach to marketing?
- How do you segment your market?
- What is your branding strategy?
- What channels do you use to deliver marketing messages?
- How do you protect the value of your brand?
- How valuable would you say your brand is in the marketplace?

- What interaction occurs between service development and marketing?
- How would you rate the effectiveness of your overall marketing process?

Selling

Here we separate sales from marketing, which is not always done, but the health of your business really demands dedicated attention to both functions:

- Which gets more attention in your business, marketing or sales?
- What is your approach to sales?
- How do you segment your sales efforts?
- What sales methodology do your sellers use?
- How much of your sales activity is outsourced?
- How would you rate the effectiveness of the sales process?

Service Delivery

The all-services-all-the-time approach gives a particular perspective to concerns about delivery. When you think of products as delivering services that are fully controlled by the customer, no matter where they are, it becomes easier to imagine their reactions from the moment of receiving a package, through their experiences as they use services delivered by the product. If they receive services at one of your locations, you don't have to imagine their reaction, you can observe it!

- What channels do you use to deliver to customers or clients?
- What kinds of fulfillment services do you use?
- What service delivery methodology do you use?
- How are provider role-players trained?
- How are providers rewarded?
- How do you capture the reactions of customers as they experience your services?
- How would you rate the effectiveness of delivery processes?

Customer Service Management

Here we come to another way of thinking about service. This has traditionally been a consideration of customer complaints, inquiries, and postsales feedback.

- How do you integrate complaints and other feedback into the overall marketing and sales processes?
- How do you perform traditional customer service functions?
- How do you manage customer service functions?
- How do you incorporate customer reaction and communication into the service innovation and development processes?

People as Role-Players

Sometimes this area is called human capital, and sometime human resources, but we want to redirect the perspective away from the ideas of resources and capital, to focus on actual human beings who share their autonomy with your business.

- What are your policies regarding hiring, contracting, or developing people?
- How do you emphasize experience versus other forms of learning?
- How do you handle the leadership pipeline, or ladder?
- How would you rate the effectiveness of your workforce development processes?
- How would you rate the effectiveness of your employment regulatory conformance processes?
- How important is a match with your organizational culture(s) in your hiring and firing decisions?

Capabilities

What differences and similarities do you see among capabilities, resources, assets, and processes? If these do seem different, and important to your business in different ways, the diagnostic questions here might be of interest.

- How much attention does your organization focus on development of capabilities?
- Which capabilities need the most attention?
- What kinds of assets are intrinsic to your operations?
- What is your policy towards buying versus building assets?
- How would you rate the effectiveness of your operational processes?
- How would you rate the effectiveness of your capability development processes?

Information Resource Management

We look at information resource management separately from information technology management. You may be asking, "Aren't those the same?" Well, no, not really, and that's exactly the point we want to stress.

- What is the difference between information management and information technology?
- How would you describe the differences among information management, data management, and knowledge management?
- Where does the responsibility lie in your organization for appropriate information and knowledge dissemination?
- How would you rate the effectiveness of your information and knowledge management processes?

Financial Resources Management

There are people in the world who think the whole point of business leadership revolves around managing financial resources, reducing cost, and increasing profit. Do you sympathize with that point of view? Do you agree that financial measures constitute the most important health measures? Why didn't we put it first? Why didn't APQC?

- What is the state of your organization's finances?
- What is the relationship between finance and accounting in your organization?

- What are your policies regarding various funding sources?
- How do you fund change initiatives?
- How do you fund transformation initiatives?
- How would you rate the effectiveness of your financial processes?

External Relationship Management

Other than customers, please take some time to think of an exhaustive list of external parties that are important to your organization.

- Which of these parties does your organization give dedicated attention to?
- Which of these external entities feel mutually supportive?
- Which causes the most contention?
- How would you rate the effectiveness of your relationship management processes?

Compliance Management

APQC groups compliance, resiliency, and risk together, apparently in the interest of having a nice even dozen categories at the top! However, these three concerns seem to be realistically very different, so we have separated them here. In fact, compliance management seems to be very strongly related to managing the external relationships that you may have just considered.

- What are the biggest compliance issues you face currently?
- What do you do to assure that you are in appropriate compliance?
- How do you attempt to influence the regulatory environment?
- How would you rate the effectiveness of your compliance management processes?

Risk Mitigation

Risk and resiliency are definitely related. But when we think of how to deal with risk we generally think of avoiding problems, and when we think of resiliency we generally think of recovery, after problems and disasters have already occurred.

- What kinds of risk mitigation programs do you have in place?
- What do you see as the greatest risks you are likely to face this year?
- Over the next 10 years?
- How would you rate the effectiveness of your risk management processes?

Resiliency Assurance

As we mentioned, resiliency is all about how well your business can recover from problems that occur, even with the best possible risk-avoidance systems.

- What are the top five scenarios that would require disaster recovery?
- How prepared are you to bounce back?
- What is the scenario that most keeps you awake at night?
- How would you rate the effectiveness of your resiliency processes?

Business Process Evolution

This category actually wraps into all the other functional areas discussed here. Basically we're saying, regardless of how things are going right now, and regardless of how anyone would diagnose your operations, the fast-moving, competitive world requires constant scrutiny of business operations, and adjustment to changing conditions. Let's consider how your organization deals with change and maturation over time.

- How does your organization provide for ongoing evolution of processes?
- Do you typically smoothly evolve, or undertake major transformation?
- Which business process issues are currently demanding your attention?
- How would you rate the effectiveness of your process evolution processes?

Information Technology Management

There is a reason why information technology appears at the end of this chapter. APQC assigns IT to a supporting role among all the other functional categories. This is fair enough, in an environment where technology supports the core work of designing and delivering services. But in a very real sense that traditional way of viewing IT support is quickly fading into the rear-view mirror. Information technology has penetrated so deeply into the fabric of everyday business life that relegating it to one of a number of supporting functions is becoming more like trying to think solely with the right side of your brain and then separately thinking solely with the left side. Key diagnostic questions to probe for the state of your application of technology include:

- How does technology support your business initiatives?
- How do you allocate resources to information technology development?
- What principles are in place for IT?
- What architecture roles are defined for IT, and who performs them?
- If you make a distinction, how do IT and digital transformation relate?
- What is your social media involvement?
- How much of your IT work is outsourced?
- What is your usage of so-called cloud services?

- How would you rate the effectiveness of your IT processes (development, acquisition, integration, retirement, etc.)?
- Who benefits, or will benefit, from application of technology?
- In what ways do certain technologies benefit one set of people in the business, at the expense of others (in terms of time, inconvenience, etc.)?
- How many IT systems and apps does it currently take to run your business? If you don't know that number off the top of your head, who on your team might have the answer?
- How do technologies interface internally, and with external data sources?
- Which technological capabilities are mandated by outside parties? Regulators? Taxing authorities? Suppliers? Customers?
- How does technology help you or harm you in the projection of your brand?
- How much control do you have over the coevolution of your business with supporting technology?
- What is the ratio between how much time, effort, and money goes into new technology-based initiatives, as opposed to maintaining the existing portfolio?

As you can see, the complexities of the many functions of business provide a breeding ground for unhealthy conditions. It is almost a necessity to reach beyond the in-house capabilities of your business to engage with B2B service providers who can work on issues that emerge from diagnosis, and go beyond your own expertise and comfort zone. We will come back to this in the fourth part of the book. Before we get there, let's take a look at some tried and true frameworks to use in diagnosing business issues and some new emerging approaches.

CHAPTER 12

Tried and True Diagnostics

This chapter briefly touches on a few of the consulting and standards-based methods that have been available for years via high-priced consulting firms to the largest corporations and agencies, with their deep pockets. My friend and colleague Michael Zepponi, long-time turnaround specialist and small business banker has coined a term that I like very much: "business-craft" (Michael Zepponi personal communication 2014). This is in recognition that there are skills and knowledge that make a lot of difference in leading and managing an organization, and that these are different from the expertise required to perform the work that delivers direct value to the customer. It is important to understand business-craft as well as service-craft (how to run a house painting business as well as how to effectively and efficiently paint houses).

Does this mean that it's necessary to get involved in long engagements with high-priced consultants? Not necessarily. A certain number of key techniques can be valuable for every business leader to understand, and a few are particularly suitable for diagnostic purposes in addition to their usefulness for remedying or preventing unhealthy situations. In this chapter we will mention a few of these tried and true methods and frameworks, which can help you do some self-diagnosis of your business, isolating and capturing knowledge that will help as you shop for and manage diagnostic and remedial service providers, should you choose to do so.

ST$_A$RS Model

The ST$_A$RS model (Watkins 2003) is particularly interesting here, because its focus is on the relationship between a business and its leadership, and because it has a significant focus on diagnosis. The model is named for the four general business situations it addresses: Start-up, Turnaround, Realignment, and Sustaining-success.

Linking these four situations are three cycles. One is the Growth Cycle, which leads from the start-up to the sustaining success situation. The opposite of the happy Growth Cycle is the Crisis Cycle where serious problems require a turnaround attempt to restore the business to health. The Recovery Cycle indicates an intervention before things reach a crisis and may move through a realignment phase, which will succeed and return the business to a sustained success mode or fail and drop into a turnaround situation.

The main thing to know is that there are services that can step in and help out in any of these phases and cycles. This is why the ST_ARS model provides powerful diagnostics and some degree of predictability for managers and leaders who find themselves in any of these various situations.

Here is a brief summary of the cycles used by turnaround specialists in diagnosing and treating businesses that are in great danger of failure— that is, death. This can be seen as a form of triage that determines the ideas or incidents that are sparking the desire for change.

1. *Critical Need*—In turnaround situations, requiring Crisis Cycle actions. The needs are always financial, including bleeding cash, inability to meet current obligations, bank pressures, and vendor concerns. Once resolved, the now stable company is moved to Recovery Cycle, or realignment.

2. *Stabilization Issues*—In the Recovery Cycle, we see operational issues requiring *immediate* attention due to customer complaints, lost sales, and high cost of overtime or rework. Once these issues are resolved the company may be ready for realignment, to enter (again) into the Growth Cycle.

3. *Realignment*—Issues are not critical or solely financial or operational. Begin systematic program for continual improvement. Operational issues are noncritical. There are inefficiencies through delays, defects, and variations. Nonoperational areas of concern include sales and marketing, human resources, customer care, legal, compliance, social, and information technology.

Focusing on External Factors

A common approach to the evaluation of a whole range of external conditions is variously called PEST, or PESTEL, or STEEPLED analysis. Factors include political, economic, social, technological, legal, ethical, and demographic. These can all impact the health of your business. Let's take a brief look at one view of these issues. ("PESTEL" 2015). Here are a few questions about the PESTEL approach as a whole:

- When have you most recently completed an analysis of this type?
- How important has it been in shaping your thinking?
- How did your business stack up against this, the last time you completed it?
- Did you have help from an outside consultant, to conduct the analysis and interpret the results?

Political Factors

In today's world, the health of any organization depends on the ability to get along in increasingly complex and wide-ranging political climates. Except for the simplest and most locally constrained enterprises, political issues may arise, such as stability of governments in operating territories, trade regulations including those governing entry mode, tax policies, government assistance, and even direct competition from governmental agencies or takeover of private companies by governments. Regulations are generally onerous, but inescapable, and reflect the dynamic tension between private industry and public interests. Government assistance is quite variable by jurisdiction, and changes as political forces jockey for position. There does seem to be a global push to help entrepreneurs start new companies, but assistance tends to drop off once they're out of the nest.

- How does your business deal with political issues such as these?
- Can you afford dedicated staff to look out for the interests of your business in such conditions?

Economic Factors

Economic factors include the macro conditions under which your company needs to operate currently, and as far as possible into the foreseeable future. These include access to credit, growth rates of the economy as a whole, and of the sector where you operate, disposable income of buyers, interest rates, employment rates, currency exchange rates, rate of inflation, and so on.

- Which role-players in your business are charged with keeping an eye on these factors, and how do they come to the attention of the planners and decision-makers?
- How do you handle the scarcity of available attention to focus on economic factors beyond the current quarter?

Social Factors

Social factors including demographics (aging population, younger generations entering the workforce), leading to changes in cultural lifestyles and trends, environmental awareness, educational levels all exert influence on how you approach the market, the kinds of service expectations and desires you see from customers and clients, and working relationships.

- How are you dealing with the rapidly changing social factors in today's market?

Technological Factors

It hardly needs to be mentioned that new innovations and discoveries driven by global supply webs, Moore's Law, distributed R&D, the Internet and the emerging Internet of Things, digital transformation, cognitive computing, social networking, cloud computing, and so on, all have an impact on products, marketing, business structures and relationships, logistics, and so on.

- How are these forces impacting your business?
- How often do you feel overwhelmed as you try to surf wave after wave of technological change?

Environmental Factors

Environmental factors intersect with legal, social, and technological factors, but as a category include environmental protection laws such as waste disposal laws and energy consumption regulation as well as popular attitudes toward the environment.

- What kind of direct impact do these factors have on your way of doing business?
- Are you treating concerns with the environment as an opportunity, and if so what are you doing to leverage the situation?

Lean and Six Sigma

How do we know when we're dealing with an efficiency or quality problem that is appropriately addressed by the DMAIC (Define, Measure, Analyze, Improve, Control) factors as used by Lean and Six Sigma? There are specialized practitioners (who have an arsenal of diagnostic tools in their arsenal, such as how to identify time traps and capacity constraints) who can help address DMAIC issues (George 2005).

For instance, is it possible that the workplace could benefit from the 5S approach to improvement:

- Sort: Distinguish needed items from unneeded items and eliminate the latter
- Set in order (also known as Simplify): Keep needed items in the correct place to allow for easy and immediate retrieval
- Shine (also known as Sweep): Keep the work area swept and clean
- Standardize: Standardize cleanup (the first three S's)
- Sustain (also known as Self-Discipline): Maintain established procedures

Again, you might find that it's important to engage some professional consultants, as we discuss further in the fourth section, but it may be that you can initiate a simple version of the points above and make healthy progress.

Three Michael Porter Frameworks

One of the most common sources for tried and true (or at least familiar) analysis is Michael Porter, the renowned professor and author. Most people seem to know what you are referring to when you mention a "Porter diagram." Or do they?

Actually, there are three types of diagrams that I believe answer to that description, and each of them has a distinctly different purpose. I'm not going to duplicate the graphics here, because they are very easy to find in books and on the Web. Let's just look at brief descriptions, to differentiate these three thought structures.

One framework would be more self-evident from its name, if instead of calling it "five forces," people would refer to it as "Porter's Five Forces of Competitive Position." That name really says what this framework is all about. The diagram itself consists of five boxes. The box in the middle is labeled "Competitive Rivalry," and represents the traditional competitors that first spring to mind—players in the same industry, competing with similar offerings, and trying to differentiate themselves. Surrounding this box are Supplier Power to the left, New Market Entrants above, Buyer Power to the right, and Product and Technology Development from below (Porter 1985). The whole thrust of this viewpoint seems to declare, "The enemy is everywhere, and may even be those you think of as friends! It's a dog eat dog world out there, folks." The five forces model definitely focuses on the "T for threat" in SWOT. This is a useful viewpoint for diagnosing the position of your business, but not to the exclusion of many other viewpoints.

Michael Porter is also well known for the so-called Value Chain model. This is the rectangle with an arrow, or chevron, on the right end, pointing toward the future, and labeled Margin. For me, the word chain tends to indicate something like a supply chain, but this model is actually intended as a view of a single enterprise, with functions divided between Primary Activities and Secondary Activities. The former consist of inbound logistics, operations, outbound logistics, marketing and sales, and services. The support activities include firm infrastructure, human resources management, technology development, and procurement (Porter 1980). I'll leave it to you to compare that nine point breakdown to the modified APQC model we've already spent some time with. Every organization has some form of these value chain categories, so this is a point of commonality for diagnosis.

The third important type of diagram that Michael Porter created is the Strategic Activity System. I especially like this because it is very open-ended and organization-specific when one is created for your business. The term "activity" is a bit of a misnomer, because typically this includes activities, capabilities, policies, assets, and so on. But take a look at the network diagram for Southwest Airlines if you can get your hands on it. Porter calls out, and links together, the following factors, which he talks about in terms of their mutual consistency, which has given Southwest Airlines a winning position among airlines for a very long time now:

- Limited passenger service
- Frequent, reliable departures
- Lean, highly productive gate and ground crews
- High aircraft utilization
- Very low ticket prices
- Short haul, point-to-point routes between midsized cities and secondary airports

These six major points all support each other, along with 12 other points on the diagram, including "no meals" and "no seat assignments" (Porter 1996).

Really, this is a very helpful exercise, and one you can perform yourself. Or find a consultant who uses this tool and check out the points of consistency and inconsistency in your operation. All this focuses on a coherent experience—a user experience at the enterprise level.

Some Insights from Peter Drucker

Another tried and true source of business wisdom is Peter Drucker. For this chapter, let's just ponder these gems, to see how you might apply them to your situation:

- "The manager is the dynamic, life-giving element in every business."
- "Management is the organ of society explicitly charged with making resources productive."
- "Management is not a creature of the economy; it is a creator as well."
- "What is a business? The answer 'An organization to make a profit' is not only false; it is irrelevant."
- "There is only one valid definition of business purpose: *to create a customer.*"
- "What is our business? What will be our business? What should be our business?"
- "Managerial focus should be on people's strengths, not their weaknesses."
- "The effective executive gets the right things done" (Drucker 2001).

Why? Why? Why? Why? Why?

A really good diagnostic tool is the Ishikawa, or fishbone diagram, also referred to as a cause and effect diagram or the Five Whys method. Visualize a horizontal area pointing to a box containing a problem statement. Along the main arrow there are arrows pointing to it from some set of categories of sources of causal factors for the problem in the spotlight. From each of those protrude smaller arrows, and smaller again, and again, until there are five levels of arrows for each of the causal factors. Causal factors that can be labeled include sources like Equipment, Process, People, Materials, Environment, and Management.

This is an especially powerful diagnostic technique, because it forces you to really drive toward root causes. If the problem is that you're losing market share, it would be possible to array the Porter five Forces categories along the main arrows of the fishbone. A category of causation would be New Entrants. So, why are new entrants appearing? Because barriers to entry are getting weaker. Well, why are barriers to entry getting weaker? Because cheaper technology is attracting new players. Why is technology getting cheaper? Because programming talent is available from freelance services *and* cloud computing is driving cost out of infrastructure and so on. You can probably perform this kind of exercise or surely find some consulting help to run workshops.

Baldrige Approach

The Malcolm Baldrige National Quality Award is an achievement award administered by the National Institute of Standards and Technology. It was named for Malcolm Baldrige, Ronald Reagan's Secretary of Commerce. Only a few awards are given each year, and it is a very long, expensive process to compete. This tried and true framework, however, can shed a lot of light on how to diagnose, and potentially treat, what ails your business ("Baldrige Award" 2015).

The core values of Baldrige are listed as follows:

- Visionary leadership
- Customer-driven excellence
- Organizational and personal learning
- Valuing workforce members and partners
- Agility
- Focus on the future
- Managing for innovation
- Management by fact
- Societal responsibility
- Focus on results and creating value
- Systems perspective

The Baldrige framework for performance excellence provides a systems perspective for high-quality operations. This framework includes:

- Leadership
- Strategic planning
- Customer and market focus
- Measurement, analysis, and knowledge management
- Workforce focus
- Process management
- Results

In a way, I prefer to read this in reverse, starting with results, and moving from there into what the framework says about what it takes to achieve the results. Since Baldrige is really focused on the question of quality, we shouldn't expect this diagnostic approach to be a total mirror of the APQC categories, but it is interesting to do a comparison.

ISO Approach

Notice the differences and similarities between the seven points of the Baldrige framework and another tried and true framework from the International Standards Organization (ISO) principles:

- Customer focus
- Leadership
- Involvement of people
- Process approach
- System approach to management
- Continual improvement
- Factual approach to decision-making
- Mutually beneficial supplier relationships

Could ISO and Baldrige lists be combined? Seems possible, does it not? Could you do some self-diagnosis of your business based on these key points? Why not give it a try?

Thanks to my colleague Lisa Marie Martinez, here are a few diagnostics based on ISO to give you a head start:

- What value do you find in industry standards?
- How confident do you feel with the results of ISO recertification reported by external auditors?
- How confident do you feel with your Sarbanes Oxley implementation?
- What real time dashboards do you use to drill down into results that supply the health of operations, change, and innovation?

- What issues do you have with performance results not matching operational performance reporting?
- How comfortable are you with your accounting period close procedures?
- How comfortable are you with your third party software investments and support?
- What is the maturity of your enterprise architecture (EA) practice?
- Where does EA report in the organization? (Lisa Marie Martinez personal communication 2015).

Diagnostic Questions for Stability

Earlier we took a look at the homeostatic approach to providing the requisite variety of control mechanism throughout your living enterprise. Here we come back to those concepts in the context of diagnosis and prescription. Stafford Beer draws a comparison between the health of an individual and the health of an organization. "[M]any psychiatric problems are rooted in interdimensional conflict that is not understood because boundaries have not been recognized. The same goes for your firm."

Questions that arise from a detailed consideration of the viable systems model include:

- What in your business keeps getting out of control?
- How often do you find that it seems people in the organization talk past each other?
- Where do you see the most contention, even conflict, in the organization?
- How do you keep tabs on internal investment?
- What kinds of coverage holes do you see, where certain geographies or natural market segments are not being served?
- What isolated operations do you have in remote areas that receive little support?
- How strained are the attention spans of yourself and your leadership team?

- What kind of innovation vacuum exists in your business? Dominance of the day-to-day over innovation? Or, the reverse—dominance of exploration over exploitation?
- How often do you find top-level management jumping past all stability mechanisms straight into the fray?
- Who are we, really? How clear and compelling is the vision, the story, the communication?
- What signs are there of lack of subsidiarity? Or in the reverse, too much autonomy for each operational unit?
- What kinds of peer-to-peer squabbling do you observe among units? What about really bad unit-to-unit fights?
- To what extent does information and communications technology simply focus on the operational job, without attending to stability functions?

The following lists point toward some of the kinds of prescriptions that might emerge from a diagnosis that has a stability (homeostatic) focus.

To attenuate variety:

- Standardize communication
- Standardize processes
- Standardize product or service offerings
- Ignore unimportant data or information
- Filter unnecessary details
- Deal with exceptions only
- Aggregate similar cases
- Model the environment behavior
- Model the organization behavior

To amplify variety:

- Empower subordinates
- Hire more employees
- Train existing employees
- Hire more experienced employees

- Cooperate with external agents
- Customize product and service offerings
- Multiply product and service options
- Combine multiple products and services

Summing up, this chapter is one of those places where we're just scratching the surface of the subject. We've chosen to take a brief look at a few of the techniques that exist for evaluating the health of organizations. The key here is to focus on the concept of health. Vague feelings that something might be wrong may mean that something is actually very wrong. These tried and true techniques may help you start down the right path to diagnosis and treatment.

There are many other diagnostic and remedial frameworks and approaches in use, some of which are proprietary to major consulting firms, others in the public domain. What we've seen here should provide a flavor of what is readily available in the general business consulting and quality marketplace. In the next chapter we take a look at where this market seems to be evolving, based on the conditions that have been emerging with the ubiquitous presence of the Internet.

CHAPTER 13

21st Century Diagnostics

In addition to the examples of tried and true diagnostic methods and approaches from the last chapter, these days we're seeing some different perspectives and techniques in the toolkit of the 21st century business diagnostician and the health-promoting B2B service provider. Much of this recent material fits particularly well with a living perspective, and a view that sees pervasive webs of services everywhere.

Being Healthy Versus Being Smart

On the specific point of business health, a helpful perspective is that being healthy creates real business advantage. Patrick Lencioni's point of view is that organizational health trumps everything else in business, at this point in history. He makes the distinction between factors that make a business *smart* versus what makes it *healthy* (Lencioni 2012).

According to Lencioni, smart factors are so widely known in the 21st century that these paths are, by now, exceedingly well trodden. Lencioni claims that it is hard to gain a real advantage with the *smart* factors of strategy, marketing, finance, and technology. Whether that is true or not, the point here is the focus he brings to the factors related to business health that can be diagnosed and addressed. These health factors consist of:

- Minimal politics
- Minimal confusion
- High morale
- High productivity
- Low turnover

Lencioni's recipe for maintaining the advantage of health consists of:

- Building a cohesive leadership team
- Creating clarity
- Over communicating clarity
- Reinforcing clarity

Notice the clarity, clarity, clarity mantra in the last list. This harkens back to the importance of a coaching approach, where clarity is the primary goal.

Management in the Age of Wiki

In a wildly mistitled, but otherwise excellent, book, a former executive turned consultant provides an enlightening overview of how the new business world requires new ways of managing (Collins 2013). The book is mistitled (in my opinion) as *Wiki Management*, although it actually says nothing about managing wikis, but rather talks about management practices for the *age of the wiki*. I actually found the book accidentally when I was looking for some guidance for setting up and maintaining a wiki for my own business. Nonetheless, I am very glad I found it, regardless of the serendipity involved!

Collins starts with the observation that the business world "has been radically transformed by the unprecedented combination of accelerating change, escalating complexity, and ubiquitous connectivity." This requires that managers must learn to see their organizations as "networks rather than as machines" (and we've seen that those networks are living federations of role-players). He mentions that in the complex adaptive systems of current organizations, the responsibility for control and coordination is distributed among those individuals as role-players. This viewpoint acknowledges that, "Nobody is smarter or faster than everybody." In particular, Collins suggests that it is necessary to reset the *manager's role* from being a boss to being a facilitator, to reset *meetings* to be "powerful channels of collective learning," and to reset *measures* to a focused, participative discipline.

Over and over we've seen that the tried and true disciplines focused on understanding customer needs and expectations. Likewise, the 21st century methods reinforce Peter Drucker's statement that the business of business is creating customers. Collins's new paradigm version of how to do this involves a collective intelligence approach that holds people accountable not to bosses, but to their peers.

Collins's message can be summarized in the following points:

If the balance of structural value choices in your business favors:

- Serendipity over planning
- Self-organization over central organization
- Emergence over directedness
- Simple rules over detailed coordination
- Transparency over control

Then the aligned balance of your relationship value choices should favor:

- Customers over bosses
- Networks over hierarchies
- Shared understanding over compliance
- Leading over lagging indicators
- Accountability to peers over accountability to supervisors

These points form yet another facet of our overall diagnostic framework. How do you view your own structural value choices? How are your relationship priorities aligned?

Strategy Traps

In the age of readily available resources on the Web, you never can tell what you're going to find. Surfing around one day I came upon a site that provides a very interesting exploration of a set of traps for role-players who provide strategic services (the leaders of an organization). Nicely illustrated and interactive, this is well worth a look (Martin 2015).

"This atlas is a guide to the various strategy traps that can be encountered when balancing between exploration and exploitation, highlighting both 'sirens' (warning signs) and 'lighthouses' (good practices)." I suggest taking a look at this site, to see what it says about the following key balance points to avoid traps in the strategic services your business requires:

Definition of the option space

- Backyard exploration trap—Looking at too *few* options
- Combing the ocean trap—Looking at too *many* options

Calibration of exploration

- Trapped in the past trap—Exploring too little
- Perpetual search trap—Exploring too much

Consideration of available resources

- Misjudged harshness trap—Acting with insufficient resources
- Unleveraged resources trap—Dragging along idle resources

Investment in new options

- Drop in the ocean trap—Investing too little in new options
- Risking the ship trap—Investing too much in a single option

Learning from the environment

- Fixed itinerary trap—Adjusting too slowly
- Forgetful wanderer trap—Not remembering previous lessons and overadjusting

Conscious Capitalism

At the end of the 20th century, books were being published about how the excellent and great companies were those that distinguished themselves based on financial performance such as shareholder value. A clear line has been drawn between that perspective and the so-called conscious capitalism movement.

> In business as in other aspects of life, being conscious means taking responsibility for all the consequences of our actions, not just the ones that reflect well on us. The wonderful thing about thinking in a conscious way about business is that it enables business to make decisions in such a way that they have positive impacts in multiple dimensions for all stakeholders. This is far more fulfilling than simply striving to create financial wealth for shareholders. (Mackey and Sisodia 2012)

The tenets of conscious capitalism include a focus on core values, higher purpose, conscious leadership, conscious culture, and stakeholder integration. In terms of stakeholder integration, the key goal is setting up win–win opportunities. But actually, the authors recognize six categories of stakeholders: customers, employees, suppliers, investors, the community, and the environment. They maintain that the goal of the enterprise is to achieve winning conditions for all six categories of stakeholders, which they call Win6.

In a comparative retrospective of the 20th century viewpoint, Mackey and Sisodia point out:

> [T]he best-selling (Mackey and Sisodia 2012) business book of all time ... looked at the universe of publicly traded companies for the past eighty years or so and identified eleven companies that ... outperformed the market by at least three to one over at least a fourteen-year period. ... The list includes Circuit City, Fannie Mae, and Wells Fargo. Before it went bankrupt, Circuit City did some rather unconscious things, like firing experienced team members and replacing them with new hires whom it could pay less. Fannie Mae was in the middle of the recent financial crisis. Wells Fargo received $25 billion in bailout money from the U.S. government in 2008. ... the list of "great" companies [also] includes Altria (formerly Philip Morris). What has been the

net impact of Philip Morris, the world's largest tobacco company for much of the past century? ... Six million people die each year directly from smoking-related illnesses, and one billion are expected to die this century from tobacco use.

In comparison, the "firms of endearment" that form the basis for the argument for conscious capitalism were picked for other characteristics besides financial performance. While they needed to be "going concerns," the primary criteria included their "humanistic profiles (their sense of purpose; how well they were loved by the customers, team members, suppliers, and communities; their cultures; and their leadership)." And yet, as the authors point out, the firms on the endearment list (including Costco, Commerce Bank, Jordan's Furniture, Timberland, Toyota, Trader Joe's, Wegmans, and Whole Foods, among others) collectively outperformed the broader market by a significant factor over 15-, 10-, and 5-year time horizons.

Community Focus

An interesting study seems to confirm the importance of adopting a wider set of stakeholder concerns. The study compared the contents of a company's mission statement to the longevity of the business.

> Inclusion of customers ($r = -.12$) or employees ($r = -.03$) in the mission statement, the two stakeholders most likely be addressed, was not related to longevity. In contrast, specifying the business existed to serve the community/society ($r = .15$) resulted in a significant relationship with company lifespan. ... Values related to longevity included only: (1) the importance of accountability/stewardship ($r = .15$) and (2) respect for a company's civic or social responsibility ($r = .17$). Behaviorally, the only content correlated to lifespan was mention that actions were driven by ethical, equitable, or moral principles ($r = .13$). (Smith et al. 2015)

What this makes me think is that a mission statement in and of itself can provide strong evidence of the mindset and behavior of a leadership team. The apparent importance of concern for serving the community and society, accountability and stewardship, civic or social responsibility, and ethical, equitable, or moral principles, paints a pretty vivid picture, in my mind, of a team that is unlikely to engage in a cut-throat race to the bottom, but rather is focused on building relationships that foster ongoing health and wellness throughout the organization and the community.

It's not surprising, in the age of the Internet and relentless global access, and alongside fine-grained local differentiation, that 21st century management and diagnostic frameworks sweep in more, and more varied, categories of role-players. This speaks volumes about the diagnoses and prescriptions for the health of businesses.

CHAPTER 14

Diagnosing Culture(s) and Language(s)

A key aspect of matching people to roles has to do with attitudes, personalities, and interests that go beyond pure talent, knowledge, and the technicalities of work. Much of this has to do with what we might call cultural factors. Here we are not talking about national or regional cultures, although such factors certainly may be involved in your business situation. What we are actually talking about are work cultures: so-called corporate culture, on the one hand, as well as separate cultures that enter the picture via various disciplines and work groups.

The Corporate Culture

When we talk about culture, we're talking about a set of ideas, beliefs, and ways of behaving within a particular organization or group of people. Elements of a corporate culture include: norms of behavior, guidelines for handling various types of situations, styles of dress (even uniforms), manner of conducting working interactions, ceremonies and manner of celebrating, and many more.

A corporate culture generally originates from the personalities of the founders, as well as founding stories or creation myths that get passed down and elaborated over time. This is not a wishy-washy, touchy-feely matter. Hard-nosed business people take culture very seriously. Here's what Lou Gerstner said about his time as the CEO of IBM:

> In all of my business career, I would have always said that culture is one of the five or six things you worry about if you're a leader. You worry about markets, and competitors, and financial assets and strategy. And somewhere on the list is culture. What I learned at IBM is that culture isn't part of the game. It is the game. (Gerstner 2003)

Jack Welch uses a two-by-two matrix that rates performers and managers on two factors. One factor is performance, while the other is adherence to values, such as "The customer is always right," or "We don't punish failure." High performers who also adhere to the culture of the organization are the stars, in Welch's mind. Just as clearly, the folks who have a low match with the actual work requirements (performance) and ability to "get with the program" (culture), should be moved along to better matching situations (to put it gently!). Low performers who have a high match with the values of the organization may justify some further investment in training in work skills. But the most problematic category, according to Welch, contains the high performers who just can't, or won't, adopt important cultural values of the organization. As he put it in an interview on CNBC, these are the candidates for "public hangings"—to put it not so gently! (Denning 2012).

An example, which I observed personally, of cultures at work was within the regional telephone company where I worked for a few years, not too long after the breakup of AT&T. Prior to divestiture, it was common for people to refer to the unified, national telephone company as "Ma Bell." This sounded to my outsider's ears as a relatively meaningless cliché. But looking at the company from inside, in a time of great turmoil, that phrase took on real, and poignant, meaning. One of the people I worked most closely with was a third generation Bell employee. Her father's name was engraved on a marble wall in the lobby of the headquarters building, as one of dozens of heroic employees, to commemorate a life-saving rescue he'd made from a flooded river. He had been a District Manager, and following in his footsteps, my colleague also became a manager of a local office. She would tell the story about how part of her actual responsibility was to check up on an employee after a couple of days of absence. And, after about a week, her responsibility also included a personal visit, to take groceries to the home of the sick employee. By the time I heard such stories, the company was well down the path of cultural change, from the parental guardian of community and employees, to a marketplace competitor with more modern perceptions of its role in the marketplace. Not so much "Ma," anymore!

A corporate culture may pose risks and may be intrinsically unhealthy. A sad example is provided in a discussion of the risk of fat-tail or black swan events. Some conceivable events may be rare, even unprecedented, but still are possible and have exceptional impact when and if they occur. The specific event was initiated by a prank call by a radio station to the hospital in Australia where Kate Middleton (Duchess of Cambridge) was being treated for morning sickness. The DJs represented themselves as Queen Elizabeth and Prince Charles, and a great laugh was generated by a put-down of the hospital staffers, who were so gullible as to put the call through. Which was all generally received as a light-hearted joke in a culture based on put-down humor, until a nurse committed suicide over the shame of being pranked. The rare event occurred and the backlash destroyed the careers of the DJs as well as the radio station. What is the point? The point here is that a toxic corporate culture laid the groundwork for this disaster, demonstrating the power of cultures in business (Graves 2012).

Many Simultaneous Cultures

Aside from the unique corporate culture that the founders pass down, there are other sources of cultural elements within organizations. The primary sources of these additional cultural elements are the professional disciplines that are required to run a business. Think about accounting. Think about sales. Could there be any more distinctive cultures (ideas, beliefs, behaviors) than the risk-averse accountant, the bean counter, versus the star salesperson who takes whatever risk is necessary to close the deal? Or how about a sales culture versus an engineering culture? "If we can sell it, those guys can make it work."

Understanding cultural factors can give you the ability to predict how various interventions and stimuli will be received by organizations. You don't want to just arbitrarily stamp out naturally occurring cultural practices. However, cultural innovations and integrations can actually be designed, especially if you can find the expert consultant who can help you do just that. An example is Sara Moulton Reger's technique—patented, practiced, and written up in her book *Can Two Rights Make a Wrong* (Moulton Reger 2006). The basic idea is that one group of workers might have a process-oriented approach, while another might have more of an ad hoc, crisis-driven approach. Both groups might espouse the same goals, and be very effective, working alone. But putting them together, those two "right" approaches may become very wrong. Sara has developed methods to deal with this sort of situation. This technique was developed over several years in many client engagements, including the very challenging task of merging the PriceWaterhouseCoopers Consulting with IBM Global services.

The fact of the matter is your business *should* have multiple cultures. Behind those stereotypic images, there are very good reasons to support a dynamic tension between a culture of risk-taking, and a culture of risk mitigation. A culture that deals in excitement and enthusiasm in the marketplace, balanced by a culture that focuses on delivery of robust, high-quality products and services. These cultures, and many others, are necessary. Some level of dynamic tension is actually necessary, but constant conflict can also be destructive and an unhealthy drain on energy. But what's equally necessary is to maintain a balance among them. This is a key challenge for you as a business leader.

Cultures Reflected in Languages

The topic of multiple languages is closely related to the topic of multiple cultures. Again, we're not talking here about national languages such as English, Spanish, Japanese, and so on. We're talking about professional and other work-related jargons and lingos that need to coexist, as different specialties work together to achieve the goals of your business.

How often do you find that people in your business seem to be talking past each other? Or, to put it a different way, how often does it seem that you keep going around and around with people who can never seem to agree, even though it appears that they have the best intentions, and have the best interests of the business at heart? Maybe this is because they are actually speaking different languages, even though it appears that they are all speaking English!

In order to get a handle on this, let's descend into the deep world of philosophy. Well, not so deep actually! Only deep enough that we find some surprisingly practical help, from Ludwig Wittgenstein, who said, "philosophers must leave the frictionless ice and return to the 'rough ground' of ordinary language in use." Here is a quote from Wittgenstein that gives some perspective on the situation that we find in almost all business contexts, where there is any division of work among specialists:

> Let us imagine a language .... The language is meant to serve for communication between a builder A and an assistant B. A is building with building-stones; there are blocks, pillars, slabs and beams. B has to pass the stones, and that in the order in which A needs them. For this purpose they use a language consisting of the words 'block', 'pillar', 'slab', 'beam'. A calls them out; –B brings the stone which he has learnt to bring at such-and-such a call. – Conceive of this as a complete primitive language. ... I shall also call the whole [of language], consisting of language and the actions into which it is woven, the 'language-game.' ("Wittgenstein" 2014)

Wittgenstein recognized that workers create and communicate by their own specialized languages. He has provided the term "language-game" to use in communicating about these different vocabularies and styles of communication.

One of my favorite examples of a colorful, business-specific language-game comes from a resort condominium exchange company that used an amazingly overloaded word in their internal communications: the word "week." In addition to the normal, everyday usage as seven days of calendar time, for this company the *week* was their reason for existence. Anyone who has ever bought into a timeshare plan in a resort location knows that they acquire the rights to occupy a particular facility during a particular time period during every subsequent year. So the word "week" brought in the idea of place, down to the specific details of the floor plan, furnishings, and other amenities. It also brought in aspects of the time of year, holiday periods, and local festivities, all of which made a particular week more or less desirable within the exchange marketplace created by the company.

Another example is from the telephone company experience I mentioned above. During that time, I worked in the strategic IT planning organization, but I had the opportunity to ride in a van pool on a 90-minute commute each way to the headquarters offices. It was during that time spent with employees from all over the business that I learned the many meanings of the term "central office." One might assume that this term referred to the HQ office building where we were all headed. But no, in these conversations, the term "office" was closely associated to the word "exchange." This was the location where telephone-switching equipment was housed, and served particular geographic regions. By the time of these van rides, the equipment centers were largely cavernous, nearly empty (because of equipment miniaturization) vaults within massive concrete structures. Central office (CO) meant that kind of building. It also meant the equipment that served the region. It also referred to the range of phone numbers served, designated by the CO code. One day I overheard, "I used to have an office in the central office," and I actually understood what this meant! And I wondered, how does it feel to have an office in the central office? My observation was that it was a point of pride—a kind of badge of honor—to work every day in such a hub of technology, on the front lines of the business. This really helped drive home, for me, the point of convergence between business culture and various business language-games.

It is often the case that people in your business are able to make sense of different language-games, and how they use the same words in different ways, simply because human beings are very good at providing a context to make sense of each other's usage. But it becomes a whole different story when computerized information systems are introduced into the mix. Computer technology has focused in on the need to clarify ambiguous and overloaded language. Failure to get totally clear on how different groups use language can easily turn into problems of business health, including time-wasting communication glitches, and even worse, glitches that are codified into computerized information systems.

The traditional, tried, and true diagnostic and prescriptive techniques encourage a customer focus. Functional area analysis can help focus in on specific areas that may need helpful services. Stability factor analysis helps to understand where the business is being overwhelmed by noise or shaken to death by oscillation. Coaching can help drive into the heart of leadership imbalances and help clarify blind spots. Diagnostic methods based on 21st century business sensibilities can also uncover disconnects with stakeholders and engage a larger range of participants in healthy adaptation and progress. So, the question remaining is, what to do with the results of diagnostics, in order to maintain the health of the living web of services that is your business?

PART IV

Business Health Services

CHAPTER 15

Lifting Your Burdens

The basis for the long-term health of your business or organization is to lift the burdens of the day-to-day from the business owner and leadership team. This final part of the book starts with a discussion of lifting these burdens so that you and your team can lead and manage. In other words, you need to engage the services you need so that in the end you can provide the services only you can provide. As they say, so that you are able to "do only what only you can do."

There are two general ways of clearing your mind, and lifting the day-to-day burdens of the business so that you can focus on the services of leadership. One is simply to write things down. Think about how your meetings play out. To what extent are they based on the memory and opinions of participants, versus clearly presented facts and models? Are decisions recorded in such a manner that they can be communicated easily, and referred to as needed? And there is much more to this positive habit of recording the important knowledge about the business. This is a matter of "systemizing" the business, and capturing an ongoing roadmap is at the heart of that effort.

The other general way of lifting the burdens of micromanagement is to put trusted people in the service-roles that they are qualified for, and develop habits of trust in the system, and trust in the role-players within the system. A big part of this also involves delegating outside your organization altogether, which we cover more deeply in the next chapter.

Systemize in Writing

Writing things down as a roadmap for systemizing the business is a long-winded way of saying "capture the architecture of the business." I mention this with some trepidation, because the terms "business architecture" and "enterprise architecture" have become quite overloaded with multiple meanings over the years that I have personally been involved with those disciplines. If it helps you to think of writing down the road-map as creating architecture, that's great, and we'll definitely be on the same page. For now, I think I'll use the word "roadmap" and hope that avoids miscommunication.

In terms of writing things down, a simple way to think about this is to envision a procedures manual, or operations handbook. Such a manual would serve as a reminder to service-providing role-players of what they are committed to in daily performance of their service-roles. It can also provide a source book for teaching new role-players about their new role.

Capture the Language

One way to bootstrap the systemization of your business is by a simple capture of the terminology that is currently in use within your business. Earlier we observed that every business has multiple specialized languages in use by various work cultures at any given time. Language glossaries, or models, which map specific work-related terms to a common set of business concepts can reveal the importance of the same concept from one domain to another, even when people are using different words to express their version of it. Such models can also reveal the very different ways people in different disciplines and working groups use the same terms (to invoke different concepts).

There are many sources of the information that can feed into business language models and mappings. These sources generally fall into two types: proactively generated material, and "found" sources. The typical IT analysis or requirements-gathering methodology tends to focus on proactively developed sources such as interviews, facilitated sessions, and questionnaires. Proactive and interactive techniques have the advantage that they actively involve business experts, which fosters discussion, raises issues, and moves the group toward consensus. However, one obvious drawback is that interactive techniques consume a lot of time, making demands on people who are undoubtedly already very busy. More importantly, they rely on the memory and biases of whoever happens to be in the room at the time.

Found sources, on the other hand, are documents and other materials produced by your business for your own purposes. They range from very public statements to highly proprietary, and from very formal to totally personal and ad hoc: product specifications, catalogs, training materials, legal filings, methods and procedures documents, forms, general ledger and chart of accounts, requirements documents, systems documents, business plans, organization charts, contracts, and mission and vision statements. Many existing business documents prove to be the best sources of raw material for language models, because in many cases, the material is not raw at all, but already quite refined. Some existing, information sources are well on their way to being models, having been worked over carefully by many business minds in an attempt to reach consensus (McDavid 1997).

Leaders, managers, and, most especially, specialist role-players seem to truly appreciate when others have a clear understanding of the language they use on the job. At the same time IT professionals who have been exposed to some form of business language modeling and mapping are almost unanimous in their positive reaction. The most common reaction is "If only we had followed this approach on my last project! It would have saved untold misunderstanding and rework."

Boundary Objects

Going beyond simple language lists into balancing multiple working cultures, and the languages they use within their various disciplines, opens out into the field of computer-supported cooperative work (CSCW). This approach builds on the recognition that multiple communities need to work together effectively in many ways, including the design and development and delivery of service offerings. A CSCW concept of "boundary object" focuses on simplified language structures that help tie communities of specialists together in common work efforts.

Interestingly, the concept of boundary objects was introduced by a study of the Museum of Vertebrate Zoology in the University of California at Berkeley. The goal of the museum was to document the ecology of California in the early 20th century. The museum established methods and practices that enabled role-players with quite distinct backgrounds and motivations to work together to build the collection and documentation of ecosystem examples. These role-players included professional scientists, amateur collectors, and backwoods trappers. Each of these communities had their own working languages and perspectives, but all were able to work together toward the common goal by using informational boundary objects. For example, a trapper would collect a specimen from the field and present it to the Museum along with a simple description of the location, the date and time, the weather conditions, and a brief description note about the terrain and nearby plants and animals. This brief description had just enough information for the scientists to work with, in a simplified form that could be captured by the trapper. Amateur naturalists (citizens who enjoyed hiking and camping) used a slightly different form of this boundary-spanning information object to also deliver specimens they collected in the wild (Star and Griesemer 1989).

A more modern example of communication across workplace language groups appears through a study of a telephone hotline group. This group answers simple human resource questions about benefits and personnel policies for a high-tech Silicon Valley company. More complex problems are referred to benefits experts for resolution. Hotline clerks capture handwritten notes as a call-history, but also as an escalation record of referrals to benefits experts (Ackerman and Halverson 1998).

Start It, Then Delegate

It is simple to start a "language model" yourself, by keeping a list of words and phrases that seem to be important to different professional cultures and working groups in your business. Believe me, participants in your business will appreciate that their leader cares enough to engage them on their own terms (in their own terms!).

Beyond some simple language lists and other starter role modeling, creating the roadmap is not work that you, the leader, should perform hands-on. At the same time, who else has the scope of responsibility that you do? The executives and managers below you do not have the all-encompassing viewpoint to build a joined-up roadmap, and they have vested interests that would make it a conflict of interest for any one of them to perform this service.

Ideally, this calls for the right kind of professional architect of business or architect of enterprise. It's not always easy to find such a person. Even those who call themselves Enterprise Architects (and might have responded to the job description we analyzed in Chapter 8) don't necessarily have the qualifications and motivations to lead the ongoing mapping service I've described. You might want to consider finding the widest-ranging thinker(s) in your business and helping them to develop strong systems-thinking skills.

My recommendation is that you encourage this practice to grow beyond your own use of lists of terms. Many benefits will accrue from fostering an overarching culture of listening to and appreciating the languages in use in your business. Furthermore (and here's where the image of a manual or handbook starts to break down) this learning and reference source needs to be *maintained* by those out on the edge, who experience on a daily basis what is working, what's not working, and what's turning into workarounds and exception-handling.

Roadmap of Work

The most effective way to build the roadmap of your business is through the people who actually do the work. People like to talk about what they do. So encourage them to share and vent, and capture what they say, because what they say will naturally be the things that they think are important. This will include stories of triumphs, stories of problems, stories of firefighting, and stories of frustrations. These accounts provide grist for root-cause analysis, homeostat design, fixing process inefficiencies, IT system issues, relationship issues, and so on. Learnings and decisions about the business take on a stability and consistency that's not possible in word-of-mouth transmission.

This is especially effective if the workers use the roadmap as an aid to doing the job, and as a means to evolve the work as conditions change in the marketplace. The ideal roadmap technique is for every participant to take a little time on a regular basis to record the answers to the following questions:

- What do I do?
- Who receives the results of what I do?
- What causes me to do it?
- What abilities and support do I need in order to do it properly?
- How do I know if I did do it properly?
- What reward do I get for meeting or exceeding expectations on what I do?
- What sanction will I suffer for not meeting expectations?
- Who provides these rewards and sanctions?
- Are these rewards and sanctions meaningful to me?
- What recording responsibility do I have?
- Repeat for the next iteration of the question: What do I do?

The process of creating and maintaining a rigorous and joined-up view of the enterprise requires tracking the planning and implementation of changes to the business. This means every change that affects how people do their work, or how the enterprise interacts with customers, suppliers, regulators, and other stakeholders. This is the only way that such a roadmap can fulfill its purpose of providing clarity about the impact of the endless cascade of changes and change proposals.

It is important that participants realize that this capture of their evolving service-roles is actually part of their jobs, and there will be rewards and sanctions related to this co-creation of the business. This is an ideal place to introduce some open-ended gamification techniques. An open-ended, or infinite, game uses points and rewards, and openly visible "leader boards" to acknowledge the best performers in public. It's useful to tie future change-related funding to changes that conform to the standards, or game, that carefully maintain the roadmap.

The ideal result of this ongoing road-mapping service becomes an open-ended and evolving graph of the services that make up the fabric of your business. This roadmap becomes a living service-graph that can form the basis for monitoring and assuring the economic health of your business over time.

This process breaks down when those who change the enterprise, consciously or unconsciously, circumvent the capture and incorporation of their changes into the roadmap. The key is to make this a part of business-as-usual so that no individual feels unimportant to the business. There are many ways to accomplish this, and it may be possible to find consultants to engage for training and facilitation.

Effective roadmap facilitators (employees or consultants) must go about their business in a quietly persistent manner to gain the trust and respect of decision-makers, developers, and change agents. They need to develop the reputation of being extremely knowledgeable, impartial, and adept communicators of the most accurate, complete, and helpful understanding of complex and evolving enterprise situations. It may not be easy to find B2B services to support you in this (I actually think this is a relatively blue ocean opportunity), but it is not actually rocket science. An existing employee or consultant might appreciate a part-time assignment to take the lead on being the Language Czar, Roadmap Trailblazer, Game Manager, or some similar service-role designate.

In today's complex business world, it's not enough to learn and share knowledge informally and verbally. The knowledge about the important aspects of the organization needs to be captured and presented in ways that support the day-to-day operations as well as tactical and strategic decisions that need to be made. Following the law of subsidiarity, it's important to push decisions consistently outward to the edges of the organization, where your business touches the environment, the clients, and other stakeholders, and where many eyes in the business can directly observe the evolving marketplace of competitive behavior.

CHAPTER 16

Health Promoting B2B Services

In the last chapter we explored some advantages to clearing much of the detail from your mind, through various documentation and mapping tools, which you can delegate to role-players within your organization or to outside consultants.

In this chapter, we'll take a brief scan through a virtual catalog of services within the third category of services we mentioned in the Introduction. The first two broad categories we mentioned are (1) the services that your business offers to external recipients (customers, etc.) and (2) the internal services that the role-players in your business provide to each other and to the business itself. The third category consists of those services consumed by your business and offered by external B2B service providers.

Over and above self-diagnosis and the coaching diagnosticians you might engage, each of the following categories of providers is likely to have their own deeper diagnostics that can examine a specific area of your business in more detail than a general practitioner diagnostician. In a very few cases I mention some specific providers and emerging services that I am keeping a particular eye on.

One thing you want to keep in mind, as you scan through this catalog of types of B2B services providers, is that you always have three alternative ways to engage help:

- When you just want to buy a needed service, the helper can perform it for you.
- When you want to grow your own health promoting abilities, the helper can nurture your growth.
- When you simply want to learn about such services, the helper can teach you.

There are a couple of things to say about the following set of lists (catalog of types). Firstly, I have been on the lookout for these B2B services for a number of months, and have compiled these *categories* as I've encountered sources of B2B business health-promoting services. This is by no means scientific or exhaustive, and yet you can see there is a fairly long list of categories of B2B business health service-providers. This leads to the second point. These lists are intended to focus on issues of business *health*, in one way or another. You may argue about whether this focus is meaningful to health issues in all cases, but I have tried to stay away from important, but not necessarily health-related, services, such as suppliers in basic supply chains, building construction and maintenance, vehicle fleet services, and so on. So, here are some categories of services that serve businesses and organizations like yours, seeking to maintain or improve their health.

Services for <u>You</u>

A common theme here has been that you, as the business leader, provide important services to your business, but that this is often very difficult considering the complications you can get involved with. In this section we point out ways of lifting burdens of time and attention from your shoulders and getting help with the core services that you provide as a leader.

You yourself, or your leadership team, might benefit from one of many leadership programs that have become very common over recent years. This is a place where a cultural and personal fit is very important. Here are some categories of existing B2B services that exist today, and can be engaged: Board structure and independence, Leadership, Entrepreneurship, Startups, Enterprise design, and Policies, standards, codes of conduct.

Regarding enterprise design, there is one prescription that I am personally very familiar with. Any of the consultants trained in Steve Haeckel's Adaptive Enterprise—Sense and Respond method can consult on the method that we touched on briefly in Chapter 9, under "strategy as structure."

Under codes of conduct, some good work is being done to articulate moral syndromes that apply differently to different domains and situations of organizations. This is based on (Jacobs 1993) Commercial and Guardian moral syndromes, extended and refined. This will shed light on issues like moral hazards, which today are so pervasive in business and government as to be invisible (Trevor Hilder personal communication 2015).

A number of B2B services exist to support you in achieving innovative positioning in the marketplace. Hopefully these categories speak for themselves. Some of them are more specialized, some more inclusive. There are providers who claim that they bring several such helpful services to the market. The diagnostic process should help you (1) determine whether any of these areas are important to address and (2) what kind of service might be most effective to address the issues you are facing. Categories of B2B services include: Futures and foresight, Idea formation, Innovation, New markets, Problem-solving, and Strategy.

Some of the sources of these services will rely on either the tried and true or 21st century frameworks we discussed in Chapters 12 and 13.

Marketing-Related Services

In simple terms, marketing is about gaining the attention of potential customers, clients, users of the products, and services of a business. Here we see a section of the catalog devoted to services designed to help you gain the attention, create interest and desire, and match your offerings with the existing needs and desires of the audience. Categories of providers include experts in: Public relations, Advertising, Branding, Communication, Content creation and management, Video production, and Writing.

Nothing could be more intrinsic to your business than what you actually offer to the market via service offerings and value propositions. And yet, this may be exactly the place where you need some fresh eyes, and a challenging point of view. A skilled diagnostician may detect this need, and it is a good idea to heed such a prescription. Key service-providers claim expertise in such categories as: Design thinking, Research, development and innovation, Disclosure and labeling, Life cycle, and Quality and safety.

People-Related Services

A traditional view of business focuses much of the concern for people under the term human resources (HR). This view of people as resources, or assets, tends to view people as rather inert, malleable, and interchangeable. What is generally considered the HR viewpoint has a major emphasis on regulations and compliance issues, as well as relationships with trade unions, and so on. However, it's important to focus in on the actual people who participate in your business.

> People are not assets, inventory, or resources; they are individuals entitled to a sense of mission and purpose in their lives, who congregate in organizations to make a difference in the lives of others. The universal need of every worker is to perform meaningful work, in a community with others of like mind to make a difference in the world. (Baker 2008)

Issues of training and development can also be considered among the health maintenance aspects of running an organization. Orientation of new employees, compensation, performance and incentives, such as financial and nonfinancial rewards, benefits, equity involvement, and personal development goals and programs, as we see from the following categories of service you can engage.

It is important, and expected, that the workplace should be safe and secure. There are many B2B service providers to help with this, thereby taking the burden off your shoulders in the following specialties: Career management, Personal health and wellness, Psychology, Social work, Workplace environment, including safety and security.

It's a fact of business life, for better or worse, that the people who work in and for your business have a whole range of behaviors and thought processes, idiosyncrasies, and personality quirks. These can lead to situations that develop negative relationships among workers. It is also a fact that specialized services can help you deal with these kinds of uncomfortable situations such as: Bullying in the workplace, Sexual harassment, Power structures, Arbitration.

The interesting point here is that there are providers of consulting and software-based solutions to capture feedback and respond to workers. This can go beyond surveys, and providers have far more sophisticated solutions than the typical homegrown surveys, Employee two-way conversation with management, and Meeting planners.

In terms of recruitment and hiring, an important factor is to evaluate attitude in addition to the skills needed to perform defined work. It's also important to evaluate the sources of leads, as well as your selection and evaluation processes. Additional services that can improve the health of the relationship between your organization and its workforce include: Administrative support, Diversity and equal opportunity, Recruitment and retention, Labor relations and union practices, Temporary talent, Team building (leadership teams, management, work groups), and Commitment management systems.

Something to keep in mind is that, however troublesome and expensive people can be, they have two major benefits in business situations. They have the ability to notice and react to unexpected situations and changing conditions. And, they can learn and reconfigure their abilities through formal and informal training as well as through observation and experience. It's important that you consider carefully any service that purports to help you here. This is a place where cultural and purposeful alignment can make all the difference.

One of the emerging trends is to put more of an emphasis on generalist skills. The idea of T-shaped professionals is highly supportive of a service focus. One definition of T-shaped professionals reads: "T-Shaped professionals deliver the benefits of deep problem-solving skills in one area, based on their specific knowledge and expertise, combined with broad complex-communication and collaborative skills across many areas" (CVC Group 2015).

Compensation and benefits are all part of the reward system of a business. This realization helps to focus attention on a complex web of decisions. It makes sense that you might want to seek some support from experts in these matters—after all, these are not the main reasons you've worked so hard to become a business leader. Categories of support include: Compensation and benefits, Executive compensation, Health insurance, and Retirement programs.

Mixing Joy with Work

Business isn't always all business—that is, all work and no play. A number of services focus on the lighter side of building business relationships and creating an attractive workplace.

This grouping of services is grouped under "bonding events," because in so many ways the opportunities for social experiences help foster healthy bonds among the people who spend a lot of time working together. So much of the success of events like this has to do with the coherence and authenticity of the corporate culture. Keep in mind that there are always multiple cultures in your business. You don't want to alienate key players by catering to some particular subculture. Categories of services to consider include: Entertainment service, Entertainment venues, Event hosting, Event planning, Food and beverage service, and Professional speakers.

The personal touch can never be over-rated—unless it's obviously fake! The pseudo-personal can actually do more harm than good, and foster an unhelpful level of cynicism within your business These are a few of the services that might help you bring a level of health and enthusiastic energy to your own business via the personal touch, that is hopefully authentic. Categories of service to enrich employee experience can include: Gift consulting, Greeting card services, Games, Art, Photography.

Legal Services

Of course, it is only prudent (and therefore healthy) for your business to have legal representation. Unless you are a lawyer, someone else will necessarily perform legal services for you, including general business attorneys and regulatory compliance support.

One interesting thing I came across is at least one firm that specializes in HIPPA compliance, a very specific regulatory issue. If this is a concern to your business, you probably already know about and use such a service. Or if you don't know about this, maybe it's worth looking into. This is just one example of how specialized services can be in the overall pursuit of keeping your business healthy.

Money-Related Services

For discussion purposes there are three lists of categories of service-providers in the general area of monetary and financial concerns. Day-to-day issues generally have to do with bringing money into your business through direct transactions with recipients of what your business delivers. Accounting services help take the burden off you for keeping track of your overall financial situation.

The services listed above address the needs of your business to generate some form of revenue stream. All of these aspects have service providers ready to help out. Product pricing forms a powerful homeo-stat serving either attenuation or amplification in driving business. Lead generation and referrals get you to the point of sales. After the sale, credit card processing, billing, and collections make sure you get paid.

Import and export, auctions, and barter networks open the aperture of revenue in interesting ways. In particular barter networks (which actually operate with their own internal currencies rather than actual barter) open up a channel to deal with overstocked conditions. There are several hundred barter networks, each one using some form of alternative currency to encourage trade within an industry or geographic area (IRTA 2015).

I'd like to mention a set of issues that comes from a book actually called Business Diagnostics (!) (Mimick and Thompson 2006). These are all money-related issues that you might expect to be addressed by a good CPA or CPA firm:

- Financial statements—income statement, cash flow statement, balance sheet
- Financial goals and ratio analysis—profitability and cash flow, liquidity, stability (debt to equity), debt service, efficiency, growth
- Financial projections—pro forma (projected) income statements, projected balance sheets, cash flow budget

- Managing 'cash drivers'—improved accounts receivable collection, defined accounts payable settlement, maximize inventory turnovers
- Break-even analysis—fixed cost, variable cost, revenue
- Capital budgeting—return on investment, payback period

All of these areas may have health impact, and all of these are categories where service providers exist to help you out.

There are many ways a company can put its hands on money, other than pay-as-you-go direct revenue from sales. Sometimes these infusions of money are exactly what your business needs for ongoing health. Sometimes they themselves are indicators of health issues. This is very much an area for careful diagnosis. In our virtual catalog of services we can see providers in the following categories: Banking, Business brokerage, Factoring, Financial planning, Private investment, and Wealth management.

Environmental Services

The environment has become a bigger and bigger issue recently, and for many reasons this is not a trend that will reverse itself any time soon. Most business leaders are not also environmental experts, so this is a likely place to find value in services that help ease the burden of worrying about these issues. Categories include: Accounting for externalities, Biodiversity impacts, Climate change impact, Energy, Waste handling, Water use and management, and Environmental accidents and remediation.

General Business Consulting Services

A number of services advertise themselves in categories that have very general applicability across many business issues. In spite of the fact that some of these categories have been discussed elsewhere, they are included here to indicate that, indeed, such service providers do actually exist in today's business health marketplace. Categories include: Business health, Business wellbeing, Business coaching, Diagnostic mentoring, Workplace ethnography, Change management, Organization change, Organization design, Organizational culture, Process design, Program management, Project management, Turnaround specialists.

In regard to the last category, the turnaround specialist, it is interesting to note that there is a Turnaround Management Association, with roughly 50 chapters worldwide. Let's just hope it doesn't come to that!

Specialized information service categories include: Enterprise architecture, Information technology, Knowledge management, and Research services of various kinds. Notice that I put the discipline of enterprise architecture here, rather than in the section on information technology. This topic has already come up a couple of times, and I have to admit to a strong bias. Enterprise architecture has been the primary focus of my own work for many years, and my viewpoint is that it needs to have a strong focus on business, as seen with an architectural viewpoint. This then provides the conceptual and information structure to guide IT planning and implementation, among other activities that can benefit from an accurate, joined-up view of your business. This can be key to lifting the day-to-day burdens, as well as communicating strategies.

Information Technology

Organizations and information technology can be expected to continue to evolve in a co-evolution pattern with businesses and other organizations. The reason for that is that the days are long gone when any business, no matter how large and rich, could do everything related to IT by itself. Here are some of the categories of providers who make themselves available for specific IT services: Analytics, Coding, Information management, Internet services, Social media, User experience, Web.

It's important to note here that the new trend is toward "digital" business, or digital transformation. This has arisen from the marketing side of business, and in retrospect seems quite inevitable once the Web gained enough maturity for real business to be conducted there. Once companies realize that their brand image is largely projected electronically, it becomes necessary to give dedicated attention to how people react to it, not only in image, but also in performance.

Good Questions for Your Service Providers

Before we leave this discussion of the kinds of B2B service providers who can be enlisted on behalf of your healthy business, here are some ways to probe these service providers, in a form of due diligence.

These are questions that you want to ask of anyone you might engage in your business.

What is your role in the healthy business market?
How do you generally describe the benefit your business provides to other businesses?
What target businesses does your business serve?

- Industry
- Location
- Size
- Age
- Maturity

How do you teach others what your business is able to provide?
What are the best messages to convey to your potential clients?
How do you remove burdens and barriers to their health and success?
What should a diagnosis look for in a potential client?
What diagnostic procedures do you use in your practices?
What might cause you to refer a client to a different practice?
What kinds of business health factors do you address?

- Traditional factors (DuPont model, etc.)
- Functional areas
- 21st century issues

What pain points do you address with this offering?
What opportunities do you address with this offering?
What distinguishes this offering from others?
Which general issues does this offering address?

- Perception
- Decision-making
- Internal communication
- Marketplace communication
- Culture
- Others

How is this offering delivered?

- In-person or remotely
- Group or individual
- Real-time or asynchronously
- Text, audio, video
- Technologies used

What methods or tools do you use for this offering?

- Pricing
- Prerequisites
- Testimonials

Other issues to consider when shopping for B2B health promoting services:

- Can you verify the competence of the provider? Take a look at the end of this chapter for a more detailed set of due diligence questions for providers.
- Which, if any, role-players in your organization may view an outside relationship as a conflict, either because they think they can perform the service, or they do not agree with the priority such an engagement is being given?
- Is there a potential culture-clash with the provider? Might such a clash provide a bracing wake-up call? Or will this clash be simply disruptive and counterproductive?

- How will the work of a consultant or service provider integrate with your business-as-usual operations or ongoing change initiatives?
- What sense of urgency drives a possible engagement at this time?

CHAPTER 17

Return on Investment for Health Promoting Efforts

It almost goes without saying that the resources that you allocate to various health promoting and health sustaining activities and development need to return greater value than your investment. It is clear that we need to be able to demonstrate business results in terms of the value that they deliver to the organization and its role-players. As a result, we propose here a simple accounting framework that evaluates return on investment (ROI) in business health, from the perspective of role-players with specific responsibilities. Since this is an internal decision-making framework, we allow the ledger to reflect multiple types of value to the beneficiaries of health enhancement (not just money in the usual sense).

Business Health Investment ROI Framework

The health enhancement service being proposed: What capabilities of which role-players will be enhanced by this investment, and what level of enhancement can we expect?

Service-roles involved in the enhancement:

- What role-players are responsible for defining the enhancement?
- What role-players will maintain the enhancement over time?
- What role-players will provide or use the enhanced capability at the time it is actually required?

Investment levels in the following categories:

- To develop: How much is invested to develop the enhancement?
- To install: What is the cost to make the enhancement available?
- To maintain: What is required to keep the enhancement relevant and useful over time?
- To invoke: What is the cost to invoke the enhancement in each instance of use, once it has been readied and activated?

On the value side of the Business Health Investment ROI Framework we try to determine the value of results achieved by the effort and resources expended on enhanced health:

Value to: Who receives the result?

- What role-players receive value as providers of enhanced service?
- What role-players receive value as recipients of enhanced service?

Value type: Each role-player sees the type of value as (can be more than one of these):

- Tangible?
- Intangible?
- Monetary?
- Enhanced prestige?
- Others.

Value units:

- Dollars?
- Satisfaction of recipients?

- Esteem of colleagues?
- Others.

Value level: What is the desired level for enhancement results, expressed in appropriate units?

- Numeric (1000, 200, etc.)
- Ordinal (High, Medium, Low)

Value realization timeframe:

- Days?
- Months?
- Years?

There may very well be dependency relationships among enhanced abilities. In other words, the ability to provide or produce some result may depend on interim results from some other service. In turn, that service may or may not be available at the time it's needed, which will obviously affect the ability to achieve the health-related result desired. The value and investment viewpoint helps to isolate investment requirements. It also focuses on the point that every health enhancement must produce some level of result, which can be subjected to value analysis. Between the value view of results and the investment view of health enhancements, this ROI framework provides a powerful way for the business to model cost and benefit tradeoffs.

CHAPTER 18

Conclusions

This book started by observing the hopes and dreams that motivate people to serve as leaders of organizations, and to serve as entrepreneurs who start businesses. We quickly acknowledged that harsh reality often sets in, under the extreme demands of running a business. We saw that the sheer complications involved in running a business impose overwhelming demands upon leadership. Maybe more importantly, we explored the difficulties of trying to control and lead an entity that has a life and a mind of its own.

We have seen that organizations, enterprises, businesses, and so on consist of living service webs, whose components are role-players, where roles are defined by the services they perform. These services are performed for recipients, and this service-based viewpoint focuses attention on recipients' reactions to the results they receive, forming a potentially powerful loop of co-production of value.

As living systems, organizations can experience good health and bad health, each of which has reciprocal impact on the human beings playing service-roles as providers or recipients. We are able to observe a number of diagnostics practices within a somewhat disorganized marketplace of service-providers that cater to business health. An underlying approach to diagnostics takes a lesson from the coaching profession in terms of helping business leaders achieve clarity, especially in the blind spots where people don't know what they don't know. Other aspects and sources of diagnostic techniques come from a functional view of business, maintenance of business stability, tried and true business consulting, and 21st century advancements in organizational practices.

We have emphasized the need to build habits of thought and action that promote healthy balance. We consider prescriptions for business health in terms of services provided by leaders to the business, services available to leaders themselves, and a lengthy but still embryonic catalog of categories in the marketplace of health-promoting B2B services.

The careful reader might have noticed that everywhere you look there are linkages among aspects of business that can cause problems, diagnostics that discover those problems, and specific sources of prescriptions to address those diagnoses. Aside from sheer lack of space, one reason all these linkages have not been followed in complete detail is that this whole marketplace is full of blue ocean opportunities. The idea of diagnostics in a web of living service systems seems ripe for exploitation, in ways that are not currently readily apparent. Here's a hint for building the marketplace of support for the healthy business after deciding on how to provide a platform:

- Capture diagnostics
- Describe service offerings
- Support providers of diagnostic services to become experts in both diagnostic techniques and available health services for business
- Clarify the explicit linkages between personal and business situations
- Catalog the global ecosystem of networked and nested B2B service providers

You can start, whatever your situation, by encouraging and using explicit models of your version of the generic functions we've discussed, as well as the cultures and language games in your business. Involve your team, and connect with the network of providers. Get healthy!

References

Achor, S. 2010. *The Happiness Advantage: The Seven Principles of Positive Psychology That Fuel Success and Performance at Work*. New York: Crown Publishing Group, Kindle edition.

Ackerman, M.S., and C. Halverson. 1998. "Organizational Memory: Processes, Boundary Objects, and Trajectories." *Proceedings of the Thirty-second Annual Hawaii International Conference on System Sciences*, IEEE.

Ackoff, R.L. 1981. *Creating the Corporate Future*. New York: Wiley.

Ackoff, R.L. 2003. "Russell L. Ackoff, Iconoclastic Management Authority, Advocates a 'Systemic' Approach to Innovation." *Strategy & Leadership* 31, no. 3. http://www.infoamerica.org/documentos_pdf/ackoff02.pdf

Adizes, I. 1988. *Corporate Lifecycles: How and Why Corporations Grow and Die, and What to Do About It*. Paramus, NJ: The Adizes Institute.

APQC. 2014. *Process Classification Framework*, version 6.1.1. Houston, TX.

Ashby, W.R. 1956. *An Introduction to Cybernetics*. London, United Kingdom: Chapman & Hall.

Bastiat, C.F. 2011. *The Bastiat Collection*. Auburn, AL: Ludwig von Mises Institute.

Beer, S. 1985. *Diagnosing the System for Organizations*. New York: John Wiley & Sons.

Blackmore, S. 1999. *The Meme Machine*. New York: Oxford University Press.

Boulding, K. 1956. *The Image*. Ann Arbor, MI: University of Michigan Press.

"Personality." 2015. BusinessBalls. http://www.businessballs.com/personalitystyles models.htm (accessed March 20).

"PESTEL." 2015. BusinessMate. http://www.businessmate.org/Article.php?ArtikelId=16 (accessed March 14).

Charan, R., S. Drotter, and J. Noel. 2011. *Leadership Pipeline*. New York: Jossey-Bass.

Christensen, C. 2003. *The Innovator's Solution*. Boston, MA: Harvard Business School Press.

Clippinger, J. 1999. *The Biology of Business: Decoding the Natural Laws of Business*. New York: Jossey-Bass.

COBIT. 2015. "What Is COBIT 5?" https://cobitonline.isaca.org/about (accessed March 23).

Collins, R. 2013. *Wiki Management: A Revolutionary New Model for a Rapidly Changing and Collaborative World*. Amacom, Kindle edition.

CVC Group. 2015. http://groupcvc.com/service-thinking/t-shaped-professionals/ (accessed April 7).

Dawkins, R. 1989. *The Selfish Gene*. New York: Oxford University Press.

De Geus, A. 1997. *The Living Company*. Boston, MA: Harvard Business School Press.

Dennett, D. 1995. *Darwin's Dangerous Idea*. London, United Kingdom: Penguin.

Denning, S. 2012. "Jack Welch, GE, and the Corporate Practice of Public Hangings." http://www.forbes.com/sites/stevedenning/2012/04/26/jack-welch-ge-the-corporate-practice-of-public-hangings/

Drucker, P.F. 2001. *The Essential Drucker*. New York: Harper.

Duhigg, C. 2012. *The Power of Habit*. New York: Random House.

François, C. 1998. *International Encyclopedia of Systems and Cybernetics*. Munich, Germany: K G Saur Verlag Gmbh & Co.

George, M. 2005. *The Lean Six Sigma Pocket Toolbook: A Quick Reference Guide to 70 Tools for Improving Quality and Speed*. McGraw-Hill. Kindle edition.

Gerber, M.E. 2009. *The E-Myth Revisited*. HarperCollins, Kindle edition.

Gerstner, L. 2003. *Who Says Elephants Can't Dance?* New York: Thorndike.

Graves, T. 2012. "What Happens When Kurtosis-Risk Eventuates." *Tom Graves/Tetradian* (blog), December 11. http://weblog.tetradian.com/2012/12/11/what-happens-when-kurtosis-risk-eventuates/

Haeckel, S.H. 1999. *Adaptive Enterprise*. Boston, MA: Harvard Business School Press.

Haeckel, S.H. 2010. "Sidebar: Designing Organizations as Systems." http://senseandrespond.com/downloads/SIDEBAR_Designing_Organizations_as_Systems.pdf (accessed February 20, 2015).

Hastings, H., and J. Saperstein. 2014. *Service Thinking: The Seven Principles to Discover Innovative Opportunities, Business*. Business Expert Press, Kindle edition.

"Core Competencies." 2015. ICF (International Coach Federation). http://www.coachfederation.org/icfcredentials/core-competencies/ (accessed March 4).

IRTA (International Reciprocal Trade Association). 2015. http://www.irta.com (accessed April 3).

Jacobs, J. 1993. *Systems of Survival*. New York: Random.

Korzybski, A. 2014. *Manhood of Humanity: The Science and Art of Human Engineering*. Kindle edition.

Lencioni, P. 2012. *The Advantage*. New York: Wiley.

Lusch, R.F., and S.L. Vargo. 2014. *Service Dominant Logic: Premises, Perspectives, Possibilities*. New York: Cambridge.

Lusch, R.F., and S.L. Vargo. November 25, 2005. "Service-Dominant Logic: The New Frontier of Marketing." *Business Briefing for the Otago Forum on Service-Dominant Logic*. University of Arizona, University of Hawaii at Manoa.

Mackey, J., and R. Sisodia. 2012. *Conscious Capitalism: Liberating the Heroic Spirit of Business*. Harvard Business Review Press, Kindle edition.

Maglio, P.P., S.L. Vargo, N. Caswell, and J. Spohrer. 2009. "The Service System is the Basic Abstraction of Service Science." *Information Systems and e-Business Management*, Springer-Verlag.

Maturana, H.R., and F.J. Varela. 1980. *Autopoiesis and Cognition*. Dordrecht, Holland: D. Reidel Publishing Company.

McDavid, D. 1997. "Business Language Analysis for Object-Oriented Information Systems." *IBM Systems Journal* 35, no 2.

McDavid, D. July 2012. "Determinism and Determination in Socio-Technological Systems." *INCOSE Insight*.

McNamara, A. 2011. "Can We Measure Memes?" *Frontiers in Evolutionary Neuroscience* 3, no. 1, PMC. Web. 25 December 2014.

Mimick, R., and M. Thompson. 2006. *Business Diagnostics*. London, United Kingdom: Trafford Publishing.

Moulton Reger, S. 2006. *Can Two Rights Make a Wrong: Insights from IBM's Tangible Culture Approach*. New York: IBM Press.

Porter, M. 1980. *Competitive Strategy*. New York: Free Press.

Porter, M. 1985. *Competitive Advantage: Creating and Sustaining Superior Performance*. New York: Free Press.

Porter, M. November, December 1996. "What is Strategy?" *Harvard Business Review*.

Reeves, Martin, et al. Atlas of Strategy Traps, accessed April, 2, 2015, https://media-publications.bcg.com/HTML5Interactives/atlas_of_strategy/Atlas_of_Strategy_Traps.htm

Ries, E. 2011. *The Lean Startup: How Today's Entrepreneurs Use Continuous Innovation to Create Radically Successful Businesses*. Crown Publishing Group. Kindle edition.

Rock, D. 2006. *Quiet Leadership*. New York: Harper Business.

Saxena, R., and A. Srinivasan. 2012. *Business Analytics: A Practitioner's Guide*. Springer.

Senge, P. 1990. *The Fifth Discipline: The Art & Practice of the Learning Organization*. New York: Doubleday.

Smith, M., R.B. Heady, P.P. Carson, and K.D. Carson. 2015. "Do Missions Accomplish their Missions? An Exploratory Analysis of Mission Statement Content and Organizational Longevity." *JAME: The Journal of Applied Management and Entrepreneurship*. Nova Southeastern University. http://www.huizenga.nova.edu/Jame/articles/mission-statement-content.cfm (accessed April 4).

Spohrer, J., and S.K. Kwan. July-September 2009. "Service Science, Management, Engineering, and Design (SSMED): An Emerging Discipline—Outline and References." *International Journal of Information Systems in the Service Sector*, Vol. 1, no. 3. http://scholarworks.sjsu.edu/cgi/viewcontent.cgi? article=1003&context=mis_pub (accessed March 15, 2015).

Star, S.L., and J.R. Griesemer. August 1989. "Institutional Ecology, 'Translations' and Boundary Objects: Amateurs and Professionals in Berkeley's Museum of Vertebrate Zoology, 1907–39." *Social Studies of Science* 19, no. 3, pp. 387–420.

Watkins, M. 2003. *The First 90 Days: Critical Success Strategies for New Leaders at All Levels.* Boston, MA: Harvard Business School Press.

"Baldrige Award." 2015. *Wikipedia.* http://en.wikipedia.org/wiki/Malcolm_ Baldrige_National_Quality_Award (accessed February 13).

"ITIL." 2015. *Wikipedia.* http://en.wikipedia.org/wiki/Information_Technology_ Infrastructure_Library (accessed March 23).

"Maslow." 2015. *Wikipedia.* http://en.wikipedia.org/wiki/Abraham_Maslow (accessed April 4).

"Mimesis." 2014. *Wikipedia.* http://en.wikipedia.org/w/index.php?title=Mimesis &oldid=639468565 (accessed December 25).

"RACI." 2015. *Wikipedia.* http://en.wikipedia.org/wiki/Responsibility_ assignment_matrix (accessed March 17).

"TOGAF." 2015. *Wikipedia.* http://en.wikipedia.org/wiki/The_Open_Group_ Architecture_Framework (accessed March 23).

"Wittgenstein." 2014. *Wikipedia.* http://en.wikipedia.org/wiki/Ludwig_ Wittgenstein (accessed March 5).

Index

CPSIA information can be obtained
at www.ICGtesting.com
Printed in the USA
FFOW01n1804261215
19662FF